Level A1 Beginner, Le

Light of the WORLD

Learning English through the Bible

Teacher's Book

Table of Contents

Light of the World English Teaching Quick-Start Guide............... Page 3			
Lesson Number	**Vocabulary Theme**	**Grammar**	**Bible Reading**
A1-01	Alphabet and numbers 0-9	Please spell your name.	God is love - 1 John 4:16
A1-02	Greetings	Hello, my name is ___. What's your name? How are you?	God loves you- Isaiah 54:10, Luke 15:20
A1-03	Basic needs	Plural nouns. I need ___.	God is our Father-Matthew 6:9 and John 4:14
A1-04	Personal Information: phone, address, last name	What's your___? Possessive adjectives: my, your, his, her	God is good- Psalm 116:5 and 147:1
A1-05	People, man, woman, child	Am, is, are, pronouns	God is our Creator - Genesis 1
A1-06	Polite Language: Please, thank you, you're welcome,	Am, is, are, pronouns	God is light - 1 John 1:5
A1-07	**Review**		
	50 Common Irregular Verbs		

Light of the World: Learning English through the Bible
Level A1 Beginner, Lesson 1-7, Teacher's Book

Copyright © 2021 Literacy International
1800 S. Jackson Avenue
Tulsa OK 74107, USA
info@LiteracyInternational.net

ISBN: 9798767730322

How to Teach the Light of the World ESL Lessons

Adapted from resources by Martha A. Lane

Welcome to the Light of the World English Teaching Quick-Start Guide. These lessons are very flexible and can be used in PowerPoint, YouTube video, or printed formats. Please register to download the free lessons here. For more training, join our online course here.

There are 8 Major Lesson Parts found in each lesson **(Click links to view videos** of instructions and demonstrations):

1. Theme Picture – "warm-up" illustration that introduces the lesson subject. Online Demonstration ; Classroom demonstration
2. Vocabulary and Grammar – the words and structures considered most essential for the lesson Online Demo ; Classroom Demo
3. Conversations – practicing conversational skills. Online Demo ; Classroom Demo
4. Pronunciation – focused study on sound-symbol relationships, as well as stress, rhythm, and intonation patterns. Online Demo ; Classroom Demo
5. Bible Reading – Scripture and discussion questions. Online Demo ; Classroom Demo
6. Activities – communicative activities to help students use the language in a meaningful way.
7. Songs & Games – Fun ways to reinforce lesson themes, vocabulary and structure.
8. Homework Assignments – homework activities for students to do between class sessions.

Before you begin your class, prepare and "Set the Scene":

Prepare for your lesson by praying for your students and your teaching. You will also want to prepare by reading the Bible verses, previewing the slides, and bringing objects and media related to the lesson to share with your students.

When students enter the classroom (or virtual classroom), they should be able to guess the lesson theme by the pictures, objects, audio and video resources they see and hear. Try to set the scene in a way that will engage as many senses as possible, including touch and taste. For example, feeling different textures can quickly explain smooth, rough, sharp-edged. And how about something to taste when teaching sour, sweet, salty, bitter, spicy? Be creative and have fun as you are preparing for your lesson!

Model, Repeat, Solo

For teaching most of the lesson, the teacher uses the simple method of **Model, Repeat, Solo (MRS)** also known as **I say, We say, You say**:

MODEL – The teacher models the words and phrases with pictures, actions or objects, and says, "Please listen." Students observe and listen.

REPEAT – The teacher says, "Please repeat." and students repeat what the teacher says in unison.

SOLO – The teacher says, "Please say." and the students repeat individually.

1. <u>The Theme Picture</u>

Purpose and General Instructions:

The **Theme Picture** gives you an opportunity to observe what various students may or may not know in English, while giving them an opportunity to "warm up" and switch their thinking to a new language or a new type of vocabulary.

It takes most people about 20 minutes to start thinking in a new language, so encourage "English only" during most of the lesson. However, do allow the use of other languages before and after class, and during breaks.

The Teaching Steps:

1. **Ask learners to study the picture**. Do not rush them. Give them time to think about what is being taught in the picture, as well as time to think of what English words they can use to describe what they see.

2. **Ask learners to tell you what they see.** Move your hand around the whole picture as you ask, "What do you see?" and "What else?" You may need to stress, "English only." Accept single words and phrases from beginning students. More advanced students may be able to use complete sentences to describe it. If students cannot identify any object in the picture, that is fine. This is just an introduction to see what they already know. During the first few classes, students may be shy or feel they need to be called upon before they contribute. Encourage them to speak.

3. **Show the theme picture with labels (Slide 4) to the students, having them repeat each item after you**. Have them repeat the words **in unison only** for now, rather than calling on individual students. Do not drill on pronunciation or have them write the list at this time. They will have a copy to review it later on their own.

2. <u>**Vocabulary and Grammar**</u>

Purpose and General Instructions:

The purpose of this step is to introduce essential concepts, words and phrases. Wherever possible, teach new words in groups or categories that "make sense" in English. For example, teach *husband* and *wife* together. Teach opposites together, also: *up, down; on, off; hot, cold.*

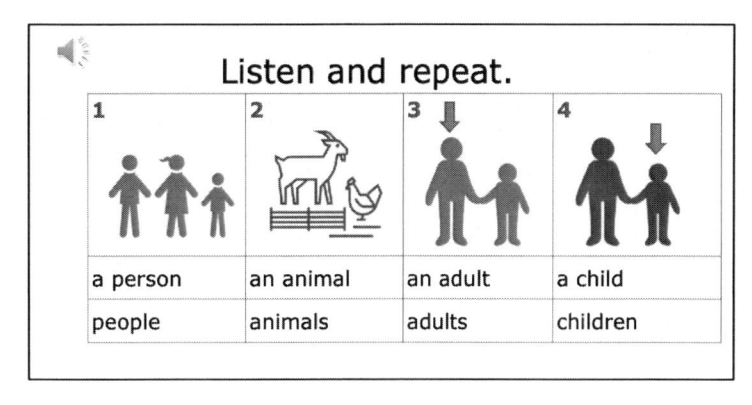

Listen and repeat.

1	2	3	4
a person	an animal	an adult	a child
people	animals	adults	children

It is always better to use **real objects** and **real actions** to introduce and explain new words. Good illustrations are fine, too, as long as they clearly explain the concept being taught. Be sure to have your students read both the singular and plural words under each picture in the vocabulary list. Nouns are shown in singular and plural forms. Verbs are shown in the infinitive form (to walk) and then used in a sentence (He walks.) Adjectives, prepositions and other forms are also shown with simple sentences. We usually have 12 pictured vocabulary words in a lesson and 1 or 2 grammar charts.

Teaching Steps:

1. **Say the new word or phrase in a simple sentence several times**, while indicating the object or action. *This is a person.* Students **just watch and listen. Be sure to use a natural speaking voice, and good rhythm and intonation.**

2. **Say the word and the article that goes with it (or just the phrase) several times**, as you indicate the object. For example, say: *a person, a person, a person.* Have your students then repeat the word after you several times. Have them also repeat in unison then individually.

3. Again, **say the word (with its article) in the same sentence as** in step one. Have students repeat after you each time, *"This is a person."*

4. **Check students' comprehension by asking direct questions.** For example, *"What is this? Where's the person? Is this a child?"*

5. After all words have been introduced with actual objects or actions, **help students to read all the words** printed in the vocabulary section in their texts. Read singular and plural.

6. Introduce the grammar structures by reading the grammar charts and practice using the vocabulary words in sentences. **Model, Repeat, Solo.**

Listen and repeat.

	Subject	Affirmative +	Negative -
Singular 1	He She It Yesterday	was	was not wasn't
Plural 2+	You We They March and April	were	were not weren't

1. Today I **am** happy.
2. Yesterday I **was** happy.

3. Conversations

Purpose and General Instructions:

Be sure to teach conversations and types of conversations that students will actually hear in real life. Students need to be able both **to understand** and **to be understood** by English speakers. Feel free to add special conversations that your students need to have, such as, "How do I say such-and-such to my boss?" And be sure to change the conversation to fit the reality of your students!

Listen and repeat.

A: What are you wearing?
B: I'm wearing a red shirt and blue pants.

A: What is he wearing?
B: He's wearing a white shirt and black shoes.

Teaching steps:

1. **Model: Say both parts of the conversation several times.** Use A and B cards, stick figures, or change your physical position to indicate the dual parts. Role-play the parts to convey the meaning of the conversation. Or play a recorded version of the conversation. **Students are to watch and listen.**

2. **Repeat: Say one line at a time and have students repeat until they can be understood.** Then teach the second line. Then the third line. **Do not change your voice intonation**. Do not skip this step! Before going to Step Three, role play the entire conversation once again to help the students put the parts of the conversation together again.

3. **Solo: You begin the conversation and call on individual students to respond.** Then reverse the roles (students are A, you are B). Practice the reversed roles with the same 3 steps: **M**odel, **R**epeat, **S**olo (**MRS**).

Once students can do both parts of the conversation reasonably well, **encourage free conversation** (similar conversations, but students answer truthfully, according to their situation, interests, etc.)

4. Pronunciation

Purpose and General Instructions:

This step quickly helps students start to sound more like native English speakers. All words used in this step are words introduced in the given or previous units, or words that are very common. Therefore, do not take the time to explain the meaning of any words while teaching pronunciation.

/w/	/O/	Challenge
weather	Noah	
warm	snowy	
with	open	
wow	boat	

It is extremely important to use natural pronunciation, tone of voice, and speed when teaching this step. You must sound confident of the sounds (whether you feel that way or not), so practice saying the words ahead of time.

4A. Pronunciation - Sounds

Remember to say the **sound** of the letter rather than its name. Do not use your voice when demonstrating unvoiced sounds. The unvoiced sounds in English include: */f/ / h/ /p/ /s/ /t/ /x/ /sh/ /ch/ /wh/ and /th/*. (There is also a voiced /th/ sound.)

Teaching steps: (Remember to use **M**odel, **R**epeat, **S**olo)

Before you begin, be sure everyone can see the sound and example words to be practiced.

    1. **Model: Say the sound several times while pointing to it.** (For example, point to the **w** and say /w/ /w/ /w/. **Then say the sound and quickly read the entire list, pointing to each item as you read it** (*/w/ weather, warm, with, wow*). Students just watch and listen.

    2. **Repeat: Say the sound and each word several times, having students repeat each time after you in unison.** Be sure to use your normal voice and rate of speed. Do one column at a time; don't skip around, but do the words in order, top to bottom.

    3. **Solo: Call on individuals to say a sound and its word group.** Give lots of praise.

Challenge: Choose another sound from the lesson that is challenging for your particular student to pronounce. Use words from Parts 1 and 2 of the lesson, and from previous lessons to make a group of at least 3 words. You may repeat the same challenging sounds in several lessons. Students will need a lot of practice on sounds that do not exist in their first language.

4B. Pronunciation - Hum the Stress

A. ‾	B. ‾ _	C. ‾ _ _
boat	rainy	family
cool	sunny	animals
storm	rainbow	everything
flood	Noah	probably

This step will help your students with accent reduction. It is essential that you use natural stress, rhythm, and intonation patterns throughout. If you have fellow tutors as teammates, let them hum and clap together while you read the lists. **Your goal is to have your students say the words with correct intonation and syllable stress**, all the while having fun!

Remember, the stressed syllable is higher in pitch, longer in duration and louder. This exercise teaches only the primary stress on a word. (If the primary stresses are correct, students will be understood, whether or not their secondary or tertiary stresses are correct.) Each dash stands for a syllable. The large high dash marks the primary stress.

The **teaching steps**:

Begin by humming the stress of a column of words. Hum higher, longer and louder for big dashes, lower, shorter and quieter for small dashes. You may also use hand gestures to indicate that **the stressed syllable is higher in pitch, longer in duration and louder.** Invite your teaching team and students to join in humming the rhythm. Once the class is humming the rhythm in unison, you can begin the teaching. You may also wish to clap the syllables while you say the words.

1. Model: Hum and then say each word in the group several times. Students listen.

2. Repeat: students repeat words after you in unison.

3. Solo: call on individuals to read the entire group of words.

Then Noah worshipped God. God was happy with Noah. God promised Noah, "I will not destroy the earth again with a flood." As a sign of His promise, God put a rainbow in the sky.

1. Why did God send a flood on earth?
2. Why did God save Noah?
3. What do you think of when you see a rainbow?

---

5. <u>Bible Reading</u>

Purpose and General Instructions:

This section introduces students to scripture and a wide variety of styles of written English. Students will always read the scripture passages in their first language as homework before they read it in English. This way they are already familiar with the content of the story and can more easily understand the new vocabulary. The Bible reading has <u>links to Bible.IS</u> so students can read, and listen to the passage in over 1,000 languages and even watch some books (Matthew, Mark, Luke and John) in video. The questions are designed to check comprehension, as well as encouraging thinking about and applying scripture to their own lives.

The Teaching Steps:

1. **Model: Read the story to the class.** Read it clearly, but with expression. Read it two or three times, as the students just listen. (Explain illustrations and give definitions as needed.)

2. **Repeat: Read the selection again, a line or sentence at a time, as students repeat after you.** Then have students read the selection in unison with you.

3. **Solo:** Ask for volunteers to read each section of the story aloud. Then discuss the story questions as a group.

Teaching Hints:

Encourage students to confer with each other or use bilingual dictionaries to look up unknown words. Try going back over the story and covering the text so they can only see the pictures. Ask them to tell you the story again while looking only at the pictures.

6. Activities

Purpose and General Instructions:

This step provides various communicative activities that will review and reinforce some of the main skills taught earlier in the lesson. It encourages students to use the language in realistic ways, by solving problems, interviewing one another, collaborating and role-playing.

Partner's Name:		Answers
1. What's your favorite	?	
2. Are you	?	
3. Do you like	?	
4. Do you have	?	
5. How many	?	
6. How often do you	?	
7. Have you ever been to	?	
8. Have you ever tried	?	
9. What is	?	
10. What do you usually	?	
11. Where	?	
12. Would you like to	?	

The Teaching Steps:

1. Help students to read the instructions and selections. If necessary at first, explain the instructions in the learner's first language (or allow other learners to explain them to each other in their native languages). Then **Model** by reading aloud and then writing the answer.

2. Students **Repeat** by reading aloud and then writing the answer in their books or on a paper.

3. In the **Solo** step, students work together asking questions, and conversing. (Circulate among students, encouraging, asking questions, correcting, and praising.) Do not rush students. Do be sure that their answers are correct – including spelling.

7. Songs & Games

Purpose and General Instructions:

Songs and games are a fun way to reinforce the vocabulary, structures and themes that students are learning. They are a great way to repeat the information many times in a way that is entertaining. Students will learn the new

> **1. Sing - How's the weather today?**
>
> How's the weather today?
> It's rainy.
> How's the weather today?
> It's cool.
> How's the weather today?
> There's a big flood that turned dry land into a pool!

song for the lesson and may also request to sing favorite songs from previous lessons. Each lesson will have at least one song OR game. But if time permits, you may do a song and a game, or a couple of songs and a game.

1. Model: Read the song lyrics out loud to the class. Ask if there are any questions. Write on board words that students ask about and give simple definitions. Then sing it two or three times, as the students just listen.

2. Repeat: sing the selection again, a line or sentence at a time, as students repeat after you. Then play the recording and sing the song together as a class in unison.

3. Solo: Of course, if no one wants to sing the song as a solo, that's OK – but they still should be willing to solo by reading the words.

Games

Games are fun and active ways to practice language. Charades, Simon Says and Guess the Picture are familiar games we can use for learning.

1. **Model:** Demonstrate how to play the game.
2. **Repeat:** Have students repeat the basic steps.
3. **Solo:** Allow students to play together as teams or one-on-one. Circulate around the room to help them.

8. Homework Assignments

Purpose and General Instructions:

Each assignment is designed to help learners internalize and find ways to **use** English between class sessions. There are several

1. Please read Genesis 12:1-6 in your native language about God's promise to Abraham for next week.
2. Write or tell a story about your experience with bad weather.
3. Watch, listen or read a weather report in English. Then prepare to give a weather presentation to your class.
4. Memorize one verse from Genesis in English.

homework assignments for each lesson. Students will always read the Bible lesson in their first language that will be read in English the following lesson. It is recommended that students do ALL the homework in order to make progress.

Notice that there is memory work. There are many reasons for encouraging this skill. Please ask learners to memorize, beginning with the first lesson. Please notice that the memory work is not long. Everyone, regardless of skill level, should be able to do it. Also, please notice that learners get to choose which selection they will memorize.

Students can write the homework in a notebook or on a lesson printout and show it to you in person, or send a photo of it to you online. They can also type their homework into the PowerPoint or an email or text message. You may also give students the link to the YouTube lesson videos YouTube lesson videos so they can listen to them at home. The videos are also good for students who miss a class and want to catch up on their own.

The Teaching Steps:

1. **Model.** For example, if the assignment is to "Write about your family," please write something about your own family and share it with the students. If it is to memorize something, recite the selection from memory.

2. **Repeat.** Encourage students to find someone with whom to practice conversing and reading the completed homework assignment.

3. **Solo.** This happens when students share their homework with the class. After they have shared their homework, be sure to check it for correctness, including spelling. Explain mistakes, while providing praise and encouragement.

Review Lessons, Assessments and Final Exams

Every 7th lesson of LOTW (Lesson 7, 14, 21, 28, 35, 42, 49) is a review lesson. No new material is introduced, but it reviews the previous 6 lessons and contains quizzes to measure progress. **Lesson 50 is a final exam** which covers the content of the entire level. Learners must successfully pass these quizzes and final exam in order to advance.

Instructions on administering the online assessments are given in the Teacher's Notes of these review lessons. The assessments may be taken online and automatically scored through Google Forms or printed and manually scored by the instructor.

Additionally, there are speaking, listening and writing quizzes which are scored by the instructor.

When students successfully complete each module of 7 lessons, it is fun to have a small celebration to encourage and reward them. At the end of all 50 lessons, be sure to have a graduation ceremony and party with certificates, food, and invited guests to celebrate their achievement!

Printable and digital certificates are available in the LOTW Teacher's Notes folder of the Google Drive. Please share your students' success stories with us at ESL@LiteracyInternational.net.

We would love to hear from you!

Light of the Cross of the WORLD
Learning English through the Bible
Lesson A1-01
©2020-2021 Literacy International

Teacher's Notes:

Students must be able to read and write in their native language and know the English letters and numbers 0-9 as a prerequisite for this course. This first lesson reviews the letters and numbers to make sure they understand them well.

Students who do not know the English letters and numbers may need to practice this lesson several times. They can also be taught with the *Firm Foundations* Pre-Reader and books available from LiteracyInternational.net. Students who cannot read and write in their native language can be taught with native language primers available from LiteracyInternational.net

Bible Reading: God is love. 1 John 4:16 (Note, there are 4 books named "John" in the Bible. This is from 1 John near the end of the Bible after 2 Peter).
Theme: Alphabet and Numbers 0-9 review
Pronunciation: /A/ and /E/

Grammar: Spell your name. What's your phone number?
Preparation:
- Pray
- Read 1 John 4, and help students to find a Bible in their native language so they can also read and understand it. www.Bible.is, ScriptureEarth.org and BibleGateway.com have the Bible in many languages.
- Preview slides and song
- Bring name tags or name cards for yourself and students
- Optional: Bring letter and number cards or blocks to show students

> # Pray, Review, and Preview
>
> **Bible Reading:** God is love - 1 John 4:16
> **Theme:** Alphabet and Numbers 0-9 review
> **Pronunciation:** /A/ and /E/
> **Grammar:** Spell your name. What's your phone number?
>
> ©2020-2021 Literacy International

Pray

Pray for the class. You may want to thank the Lord for your students, their learning, and for his eternal love.

Preview

Students need to be able to read and write in their native language and know the English letters and numbers 0-9 as a prerequisite for this course. This lesson reviews the letters and numbers to make sure they understand them well.

Students who do not know the English letters and numbers may need to practice this lesson several times. They can also be taught with the *Firm Foundations* Pre-Reader and Books available from LiteracyInternational.net. Students who cannot read and write in their native language can first be taught with native language primers available from LiteracyInternational.net

What do you see?

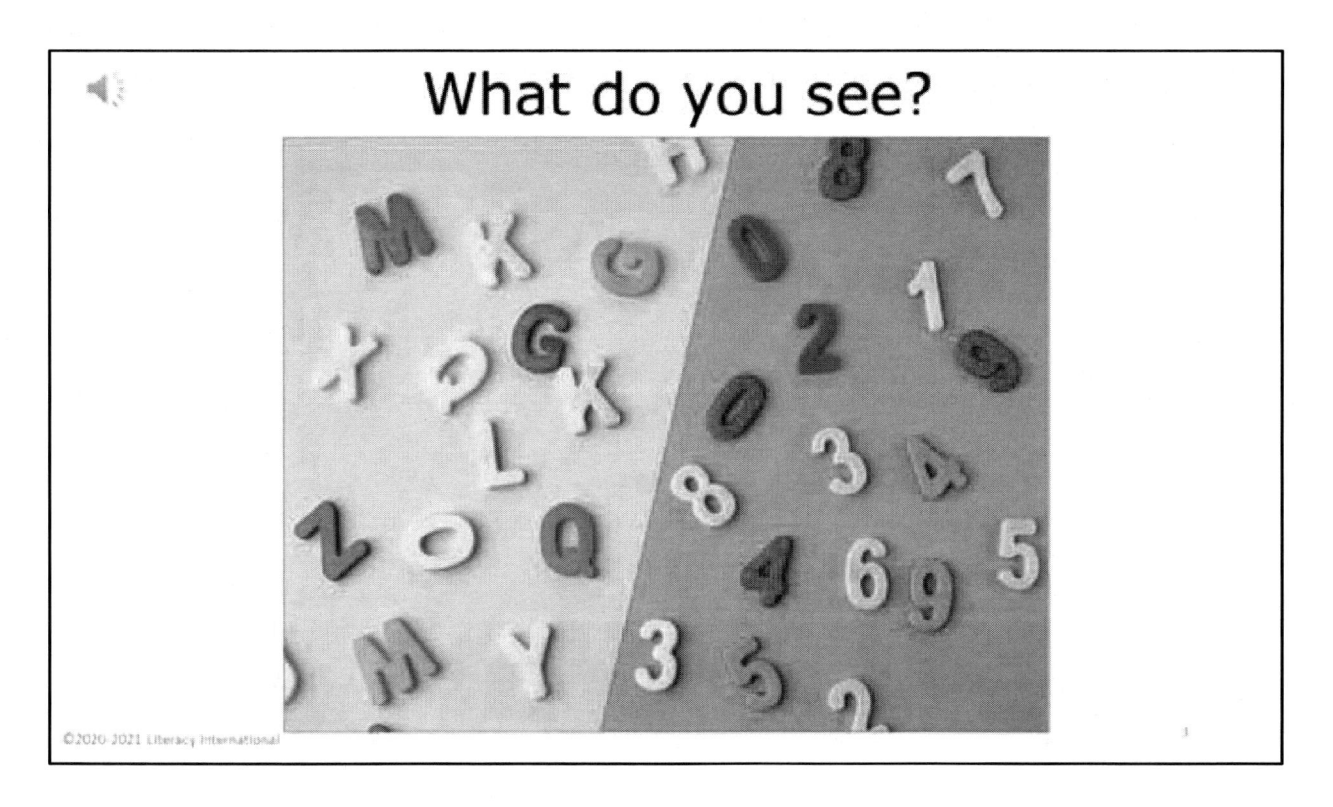

1A. Discuss Theme Picture

- Ask "What do you see in this picture?" and "What else?" to elicit vocabulary they already know.
- Repeat their answers and write, or show their words on the next slide.
- Use English only as much as possible.

Answers may include: letters, numbers, alphabet, M, K, 3, 4, etc.

More advanced students can be encouraged to make complete sentences:
"There are many letters. The number 3 is yellow."

What do you see?

Letters   Numbers

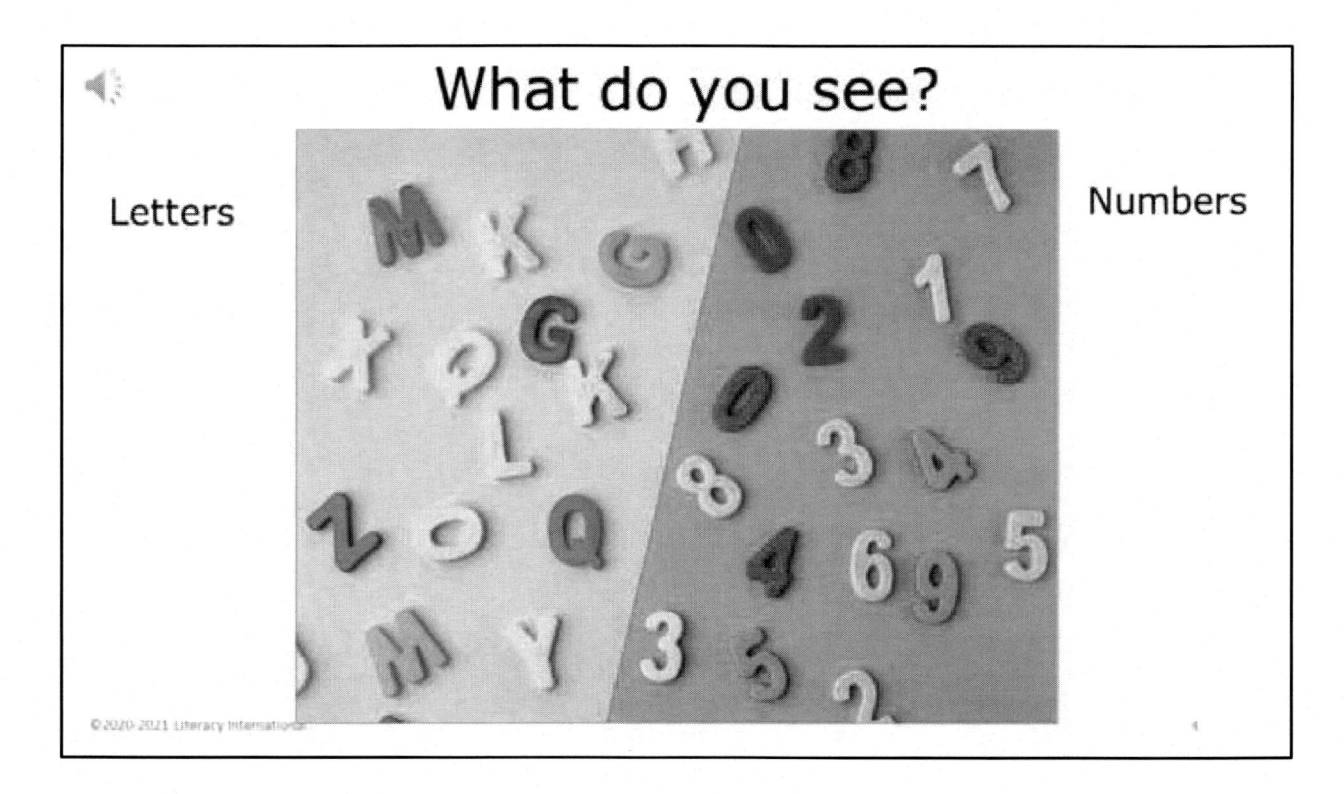

1A. Discuss Theme Picture

Please show the names of the theme picture items to the students briefly.
These words can be studied for homework.
Practice of vocabulary begins with the following slide.

Listen and repeat.

ABCDEFGH IJKLMNOP QRSTUVW XYZ	0123456789	Adam	A-d-a-m
a letter	a number	to say	to spell
letters	numbers	Please say your name.	Please spell your name.

2. Vocabulary – You may use letter and number cards and nametags to demonstrate.

1. **Say the new words in a simple sentence:** "This is a letter." several times, while pointing. "These are letters." Students just watch and listen. Be sure to use a natural speaking voice, and good rhythm and intonation.

2. **Say the word and the article that goes with it several times**, as you indicate the object. For example, say: *a letter, a letter, a letter*. Have your students then repeat the word after you several times.

3. **Say the word in the same sentence again**. Have students repeat after you each time, "This is a letter."

4. **Check students' comprehension by asking direct questions**. For example, *What is this? Is this a number?*

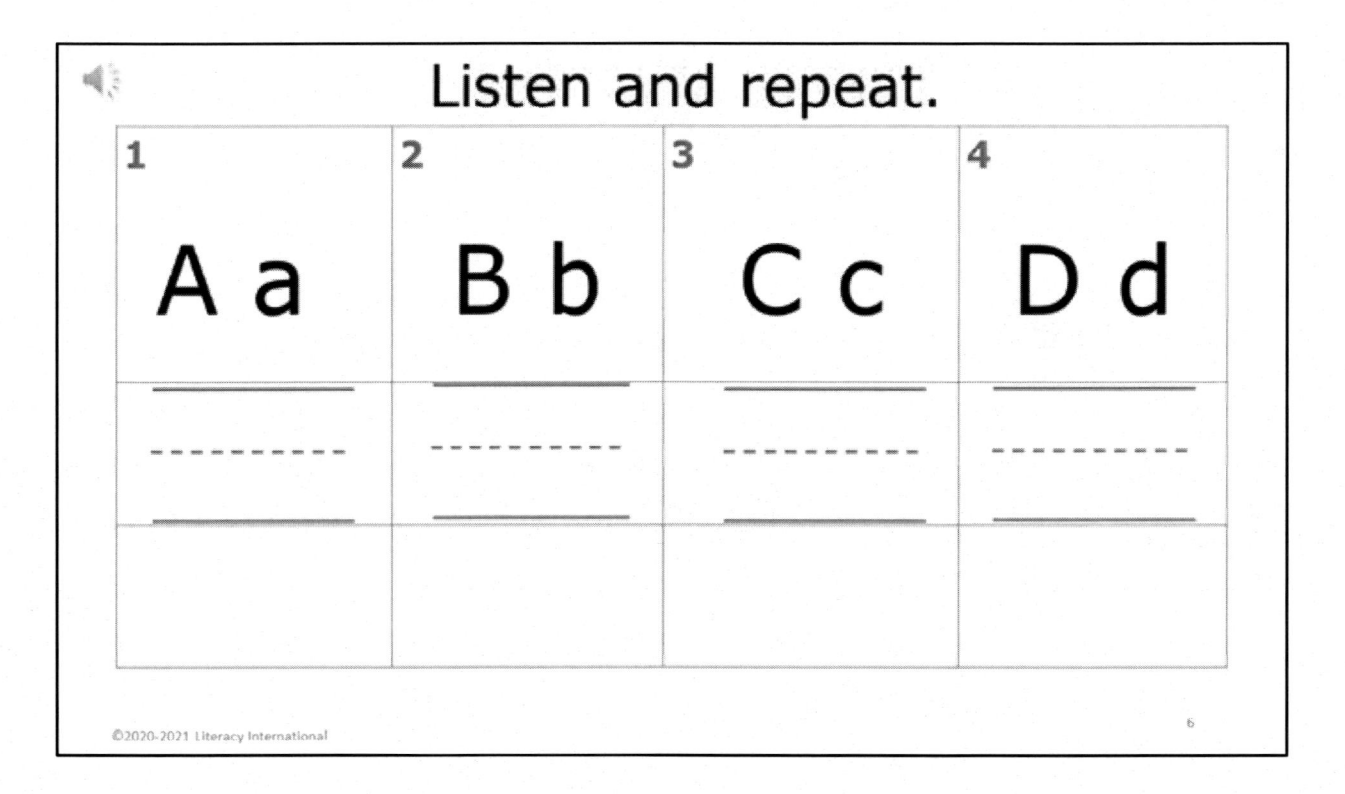

Listen and repeat.

1	2	3	4
A a	B b	C c	D d

2. Vocabulary – The alphabet

1. Model: Say the letter several times, while pointing to it. For example, "A, A, A." Be sure to use a natural speaking voice, and good rhythm and intonation. Students just watch and listen.

2. Repeat: Say the letter again while you point and ask students to repeat after you.

3. Solo: Ask individual students to say the letters.

4. Check students' comprehension by asking direct questions. For example, *What is this? Is this A?*

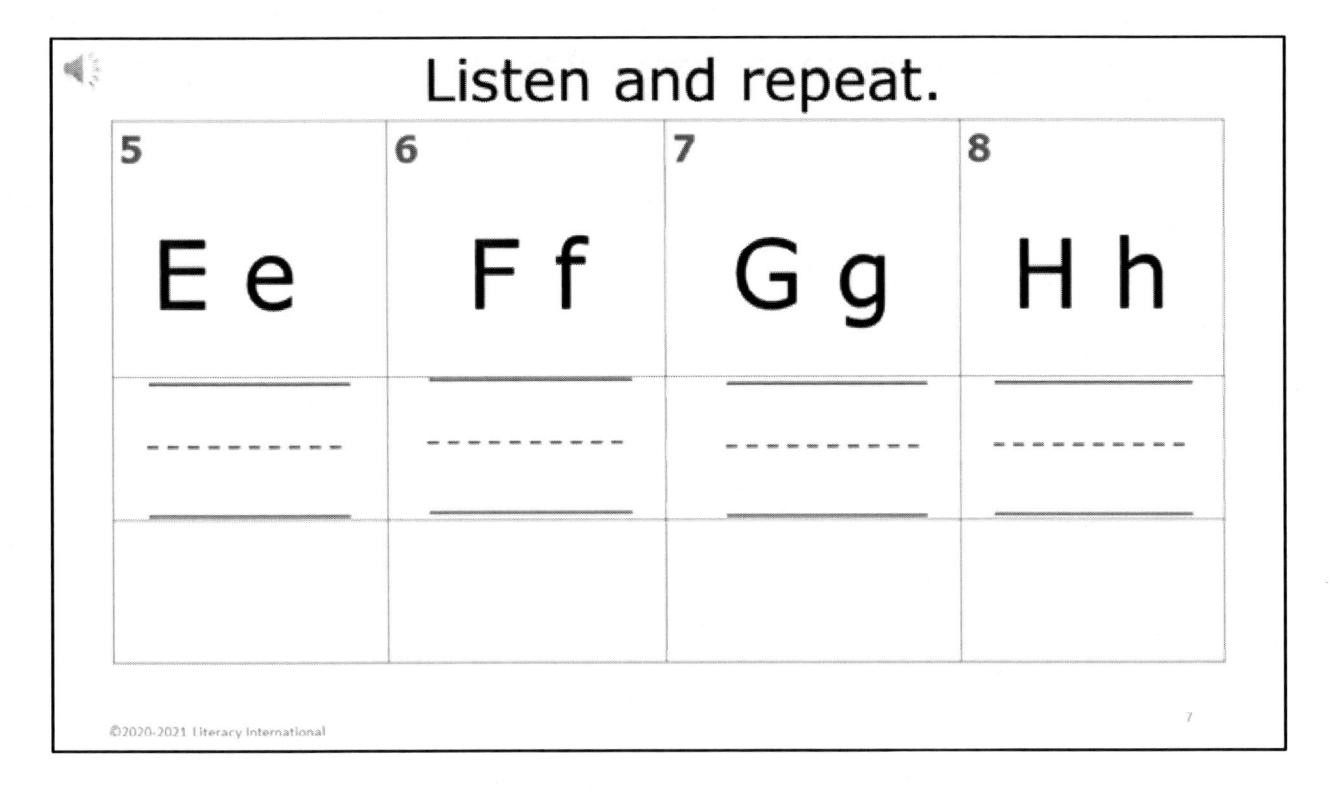

Listen and repeat.

5	6	7	8
E e	F f	G g	H h

2. Vocabulary

1. Model: Say the letter several times, while pointing to it. For example, "A, A, A." Be sure to use a natural speaking voice, and good rhythm and intonation. Students just watch and listen.

2. Repeat: Say the letter again while you point and ask students to repeat after you.

3. Solo: Ask individual students to say the letters.

4. Check students' comprehension by asking direct questions. For example, *What is this? Is this A?*

9	10	11	12
I i	J j	K k	L l

Listen and repeat.

2. Vocabulary

1. Model: Say the letter several times, while pointing to it. For example, "A, A, A." Be sure to use a natural speaking voice, and good rhythm and intonation. Students just watch and listen.

2. Repeat: Say the letter again while you point and ask students to repeat after you.

3. Solo: Ask individual students to say the letters.

4. Check students' comprehension by asking direct questions. For example, *What is this? Is this A?*

Listen and repeat.

13	14	15	16
M m	N n	O o	P p

2. Vocabulary

1. Model: Say the letter several times, while pointing to it. For example, "A, A, A." Be sure to use a natural speaking voice, and good rhythm and intonation. Students just watch and listen.

2. Repeat: Say the letter again while you point and ask students to repeat after you.

3. Solo: Ask individual students to say the letters.

4. Check students' comprehension by asking direct questions. For example, *What is this? Is this A?*

> # Listen and repeat.
>
> | 17 | 18 | 19 | 20 |
> |---|---|---|---|
> | Q q | R r | S s | T t |

2. Vocabulary

1. Model: Say the letter several times, while pointing to it. For example, "A, A, A." Be sure to use a natural speaking voice, and good rhythm and intonation. Students just watch and listen.

2. Repeat: Say the letter again while you point and ask students to repeat after you.

3. Solo: Ask individual students to say the letters.

4. Check students' comprehension by asking direct questions. For example, *What is this? Is this A?*

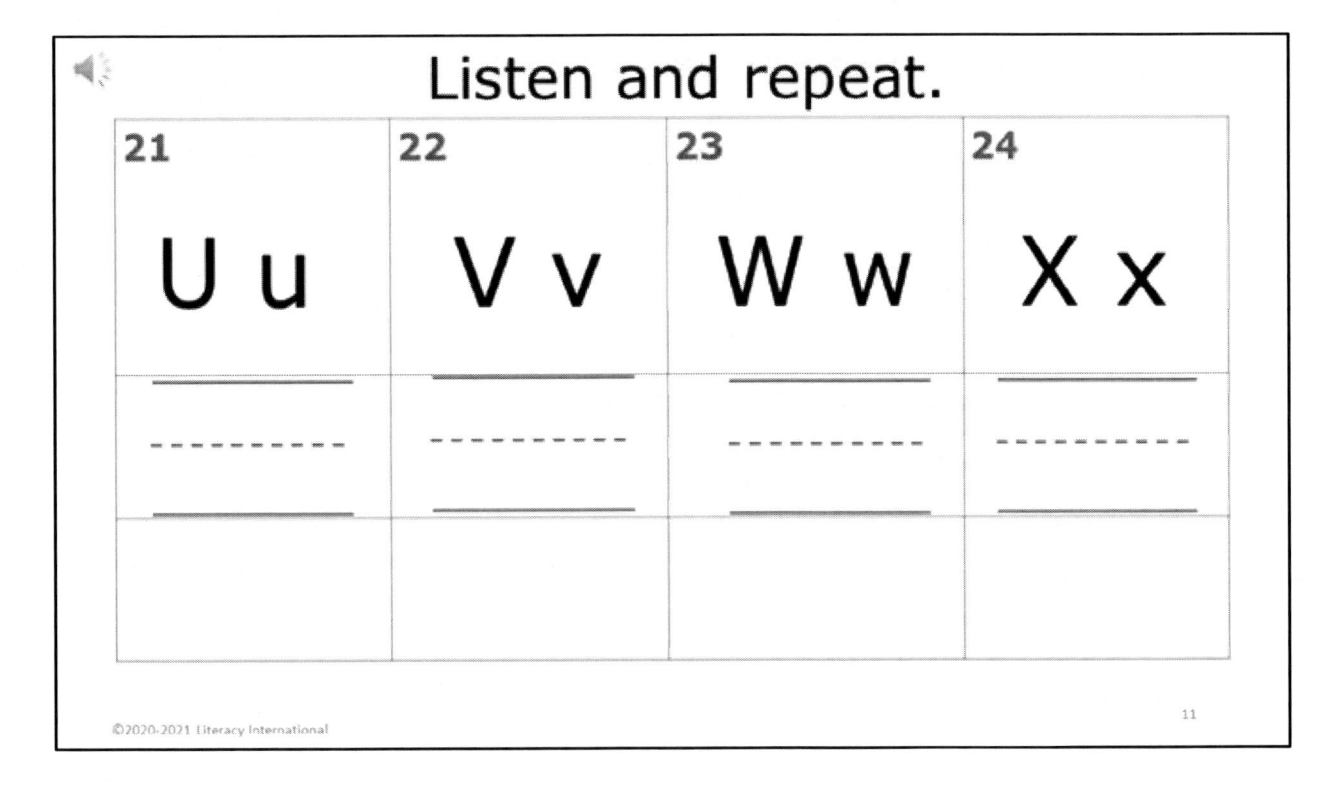

Listen and repeat.

21	22	23	24
U u	V v	W w	X x

2. Vocabulary

1. Model: Say the letter several times, while pointing to it. For example, "A, A, A." Be sure to use a natural speaking voice, and good rhythm and intonation. Students just watch and listen.

2. Repeat: Say the letter again while you point and ask students to repeat after you.

3. Solo: Ask individual students to say the letters.

4. Check students' comprehension by asking direct questions. For example, *What is this? Is this A?*

| 25 Y y | 26 Z z | 0 zero | 1 one |

Listen and repeat.

2. Vocabulary – The alphabet and numbers

Note, the number "zero" may also be shortened to "O."

1. Model: Say the letter or number several times, while pointing to it. For example, "1,1,1." Be sure to use a natural speaking voice, and good rhythm and intonation. Students just watch and listen.

2. Repeat: Say the letter or number again while you point and ask students to repeat after you.

3. Solo: Ask individual students to say the letters.

4. Check students' comprehension by asking direct questions. For example, *What is this? Is this 1?*

Listen and repeat.

2	3	4	5
two	three	four	five

2. Vocabulary

1. Model: Say the number several times, while pointing to it. For example, "1,1,1." Be sure to use a natural speaking voice, and good rhythm and intonation. Students just watch and listen.

2. Repeat: Say the number again while you point and ask students to repeat after you.

3. Solo: Ask individual students to say the numbers.

4. Check students' comprehension by asking direct questions. For example, *What is this? Is this 5?*

Listen and repeat.

6	7	8	9
six	seven	eight	nine

2. Vocabulary

1. Model: Say the number several times, while pointing to it. For example, "1,1,1." Be sure to use a natural speaking voice, and good rhythm and intonation. Students just watch and listen.

2. Repeat: Say the number again while you point and ask students to repeat after you.

3. Solo: Ask individual students to say the numbers.

4. Check students' comprehension by asking direct questions. For example, *What is this? Is this 5?*

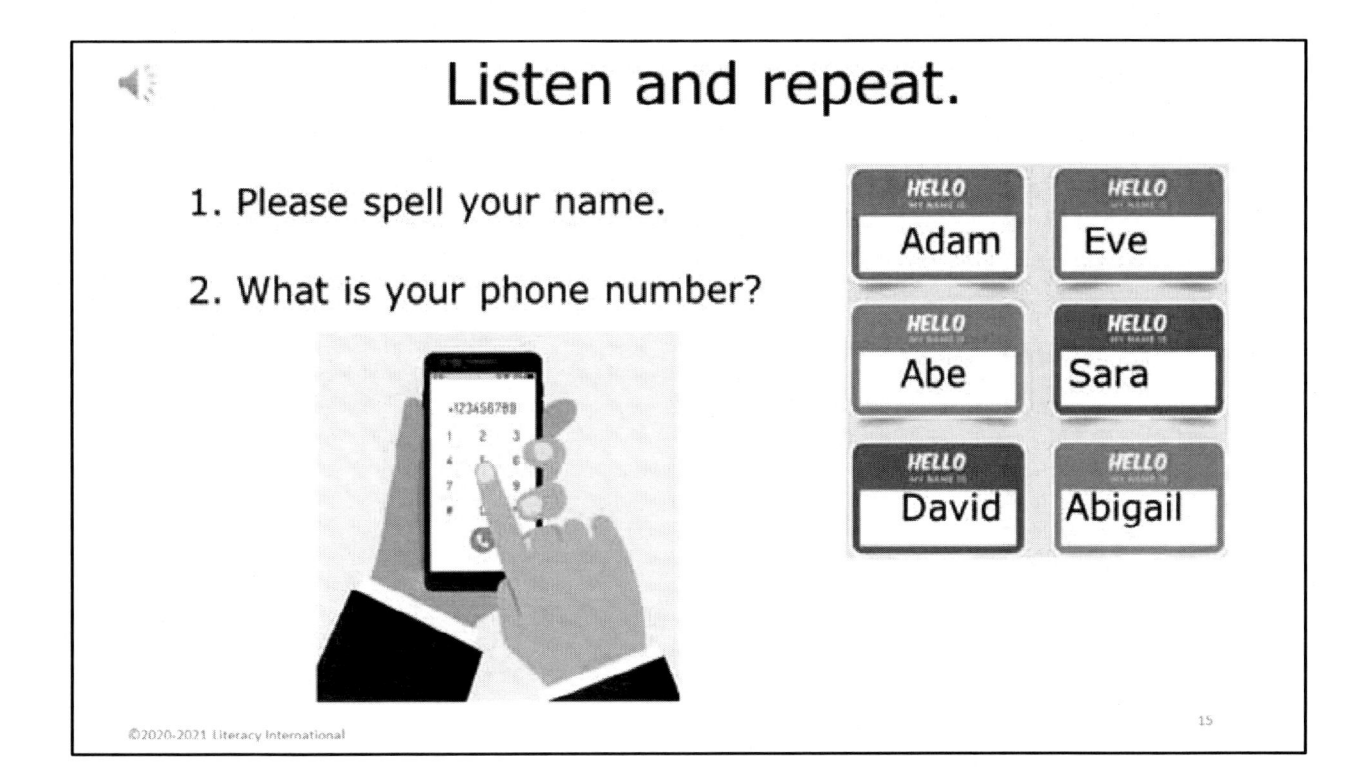

> **Listen and repeat.**
>
> 1. Please spell your name.
> 2. What is your phone number?
>
> HELLO Adam | HELLO Eve
> HELLO Abe | HELLO Sara
> HELLO David | HELLO Abigail

2B. Grammar

Model, Repeat, and Solo the pronunciation of these phrases.
Demonstrate spelling your name and giving your phone number to the class.
You may also spell the names on your students' nametags and/or the nametags in the picture.

01-15

> # Listen and repeat.
>
> A: What's your name?
> B: Adam.
> A: Please spell your name.
> B: A-d-a-m.
> A: What's your phone number?
> B: 312-555-7890.
> A: Thank you!
>
> ©2020-2021 Literacy International

3A. Conversation 1:

1. Model: Say both parts of the conversation several times. Use A and B cards, stick figures, or change your physical position to indicate the dual parts. Role play the parts to convey the meaning of the conversation. **Students are to watch and listen.**

2. Repeat: Say one line at a time and have students repeat until they can be understood.

3. Solo: You begin the conversation and call on individual students to respond. Then reverse the roles (students are A, you are B).

4. Once students can do both parts, **encourage free conversation** (students substitute the blue words and answer truthfully).

01-16

Listen and repeat.

1. /A/	2. /E/
J	B
H	C
A	G
K	T
8	3

4A. Pronunciation sounds – Long /A/ and Long /E/

1. **Model: Say the sound several times while pointing to it.** (For example, point to the **A** and say /A/ /A/ /A/ . **Then say the sound and quickly read the entire list, pointing to each item as you read it** (/A/ J, H, A, K, 8). Students just watch and listen.

2. **Repeat: Say the sound and each example several times, having students repeat each time after you in unison.** Be sure to use your normal voice and rate of speed. Do one column at a time, top to bottom.

3. **Solo: Call on individuals to say a sound and its group.** Give lots of praise.

Listen and repeat.

—	—
	-
say	letter
spell	number
phone	seven
name	listen
see	thank you

4B. Pronunciation - Hum and clap the stress.

Begin by humming the stress of a column of words. Hum higher, longer and louder for big dashes, lower, shorter and quieter for small dashes.

You may use hand gestures to indicate that **the stressed syllable is higher in pitch, longer in duration and louder.** Invite your students to join in humming the rhythm. Once the class is humming the rhythm in unison, you can begin saying the words. You may also wish to clap the syllables while you say the words.

1. Model: Hum and then say each word in the group several times. Students listen.
2. Repeat: students repeat words after you in unison.
3. Solo: call on individuals to read the entire group of words.

> # God is Love
> 1 John 4:16 ERV
>
> So we know the love that God has for us, and we trust that love.
>
> God is love. Everyone who lives in love lives in God, and God lives in them.

5: Bible Reading

First help students to find and read 1 John 4:16 in their own language so they understand it. www.Bible.is, ScriptureEarth.org and BibleGateway.com have many languages. (Note, there are 4 books named "John" in the Bible. This is from **1 John** near the end of the Bible, after 2 Peter). The hyperlink of the Bible verse will take you to https://live.bible.is/ where you can select from over 1,000 languages to read and listen to the verse.

A. Read the verse out loud to the class in English.
B. If students ask about specific words, give simple definitions or translate.
C. Ask volunteers to read aloud sentences.
D. Ask if they have any questions or comments about the verse or picture. The picture is a father who loves and forgives his son.

> **Listen and write the letters and numbers.**

1.	
2.	
3.	
4.	
5.	
6.	
7.	

spell
3456
012
name
say
789
ABC

6A Activities – Dictation

Read the sets of letters and numbers slowly three times. Do not say the words, just spell them. Students will write them just one time on each line.

For more advanced students, you may hide the word list by making the font white or covering it.

1. A-B-C, A-B-C, A-B-C
2. S-A-Y, S-A-Y, S-A-Y
3. 0-1-2, 0-1-2, 0-1-2
4. 7-8-9, 7-8-9, 7-8-9
5. S-P-E-L-L, S-P-E-L-L, S-P-E-L-L
6. N-A-M-E, N-A-M-E, N-A-M-E
7. 3-4-5-6, 3-4-5-6, 3-4-5-6

Write questions and ask your partner.

Questions	Answers
1. What's your teacher's name?	
2. What's your _____?	
3. Please spell your _____.	
4. What's your phone _____?	

6B Activities – Pair work

Ask students to complete writing the questions with their own words. Number 1 is an example.

Their questions will vary, but may include:
2. What's your name?
3. Please spell your name
4. What's your phone number?

Then ask students to interview a partner, and write their partner's answers. Then they will switch roles and answer their partner's questions.
Check answers for correct spelling.

Say the letters and numbers

CALIFORNIA DNH 3289 NATIONAL PARK
ILLINOIS 39-H957 Big Truck
PENNSYLVANIA DSM 9067
NEDERLAND FTN : 2800
FLORIDA 621J357 SUNSHINE STATE

JKR : 0058 CALIFORNIA
ARIZONA JAF 4852 GRAND CANYON STATE
ARIZONA GLR 154
HAWAII FN3596 ALOHA
TYI 415 OREGON

COLORADO A49 358 Big Truck
USA A35-483 State of New York
MONTANA NSY · 5831
CANADA SN 0258 CONFEDERATION
RIO DE JANERO FTS 053

ILLINOIS BUN 1648
HSN E9 FUR : 2896
HAWAII DFY-14-12 ALOHA STATE
MONTANA JKR:0058
California 3E-6583 PALM BEACH COUNTY
W2UFQ WASHINGTON

Find 3 License Plates

©2020-2021 Literacy International

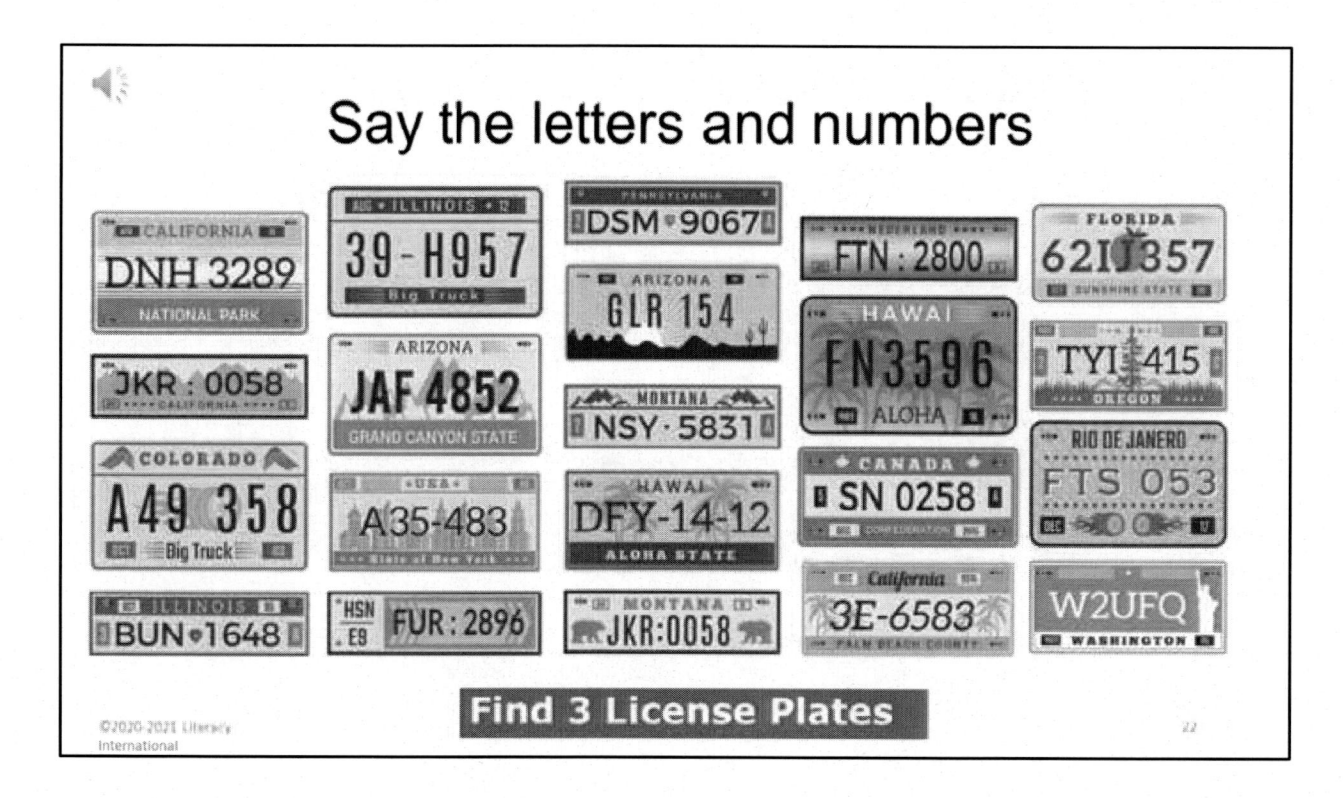

6C. Activities - Pair work.

Ask the students to say the letters and numbers of 3 license plates to their partner. The partner must point to (or circle) the correct license plate.

Then switch, and partner B describes the picture while partner A points.

Model by giving an example, say "GLR 154." Repeat if needed. Students should point to the yellow Arizona plate.

01-22

> **Sing the alphabet song!**
>
> A-B-C-D-E-F-G
> H-I-J-K-L-M-N-O-P
> Q-R-S
> T-U-V
> W-X
> Y and Z
> Our Lord is the A to Z
> He loves us eternally.

7. Song

Students will learn the song and may also sing other songs, if time permits.

1. Model: Read the song lyrics out loud to the class. Ask if there are any questions. Write on board words that students ask about and give simple definitions Then sing it two or three times, as the students just listen.

2. Repeat: sing the selection again, a line or sentence at a time, as students repeat after you. Then play the recording and sing the song together as a class in unison.

3. Solo: The student sings solo (or if shy, can just read the words aloud).

> # 1 & 2 Homework
>
> 1. Read the next lesson's Bible verses: Isaiah 54:10 and Luke 15:20 in your language.
>
> 2. Fill in the blanks:
>
> A. My name is _____.
>
> B. My phone number is _____.
>
> C. My teacher's name is _____.
>
> D. The numbers are 0,1,___,3,4,___,6,7,___,9
>
> E. The letters are A,B,C,___,E,F,G,___,I,J,K,___,M,N,O,___

Homework 1, and 2 - Reading the next Bible Lesson in L1, and writing

Students will always read the Bible lesson in their first language (L1) before reading it in English for the next lesson. Help them get a Bible in their own language if they don't have one. They may also use Bible.is, BibleGateway.com, or other Bible translation resources. The hyperlink of the Bible verses connects to https://live.bible.is where students can select from over 1,000 languages to read and listen to the verses.

Model. Go over all **homework assignments** to be sure students understand what to do.
Repeat. Encourage students to find someone with whom to practice conversing and reading the completed homework assignment. They may use a bilingual dictionary.
Solo. Students will turn in their work to you. Be sure to check it, including spelling. Explain mistakes, and give them praise and encouragement.

3. Homework. Write the words and numbers.

ABCDEFGHIJK LMNOPQRSTU VW XYZ	0123456 789	Adam	A-d-a-m	zero	nine
a letter					
letters					
two	seven	three	five	one	eight
					8
					eight

Homework 3. – Write the vocabulary words with the pictures
This homework practices writing the vocabulary. The first and last boxes are examples.
1. a letter, letters
2. a number, numbers
3. to say, Say your name.
4. to spell, Spell your name.
5. 0, zero
6. 9, nine
7. 2, two
8. 7, seven
9. 3, three
10. 5, five
11. 1, one
12. 8, eight

01-25

> # 4. Homework
>
> Watch and listen to slides 27-52.
>
> Then write and say the letters and numbers on slides 6-14.
>
> ©2020 Literacy International

Homework 4 – Write and say the letters and numbers.

This homework practices writing, spelling and pronouncing the letters and numbers.

Slides 27-54 are animated, narrated slides which demonstrate handwriting and sounds. Play the slideshow and ask if students have questions before doing their writing homework.

Students may write their work on slides 6-14 or on paper or a digital document.

a - apple

Laughing Letters on slides 27-52 © 2020 Easy Breezy Reading and used with permission. Visit EasyReadEnglish.com for more resources.

b - bat & ball

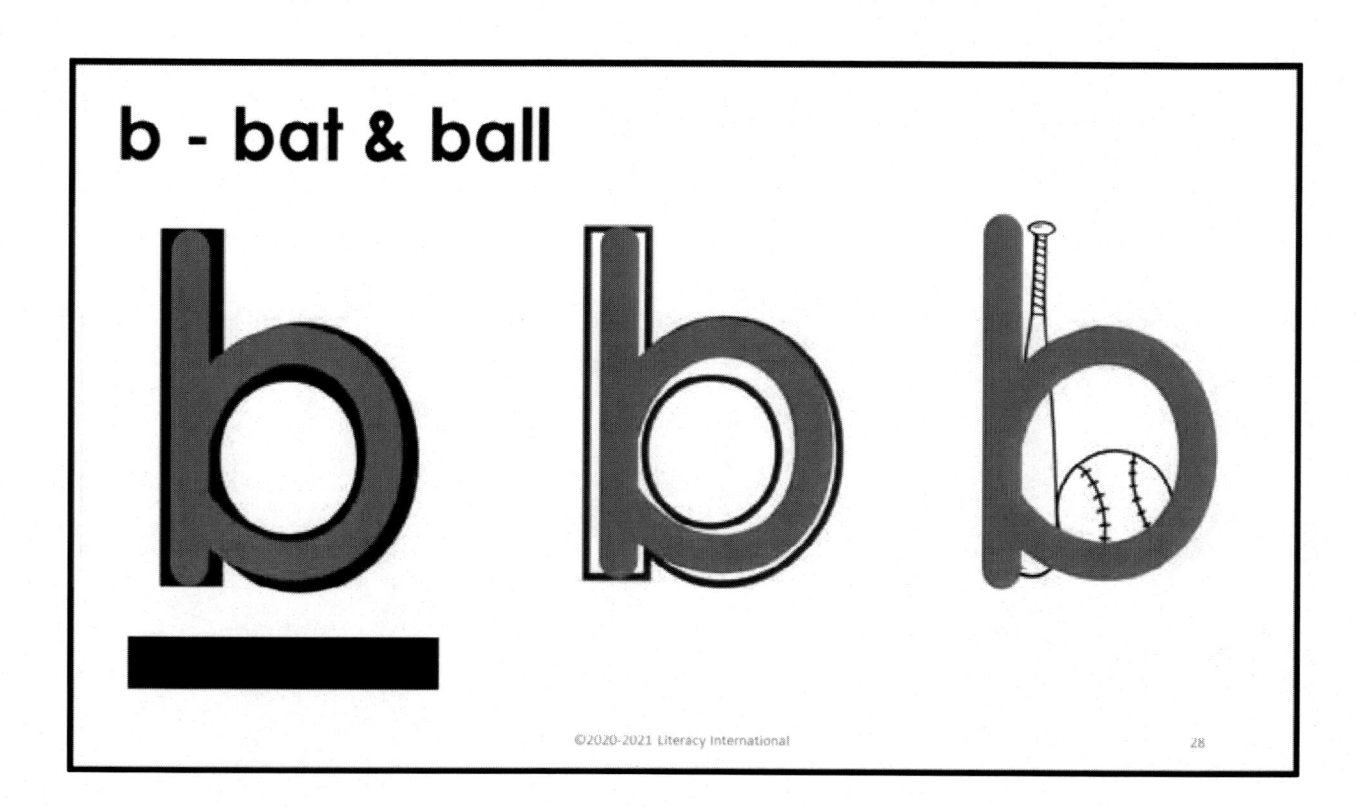

c - cookie

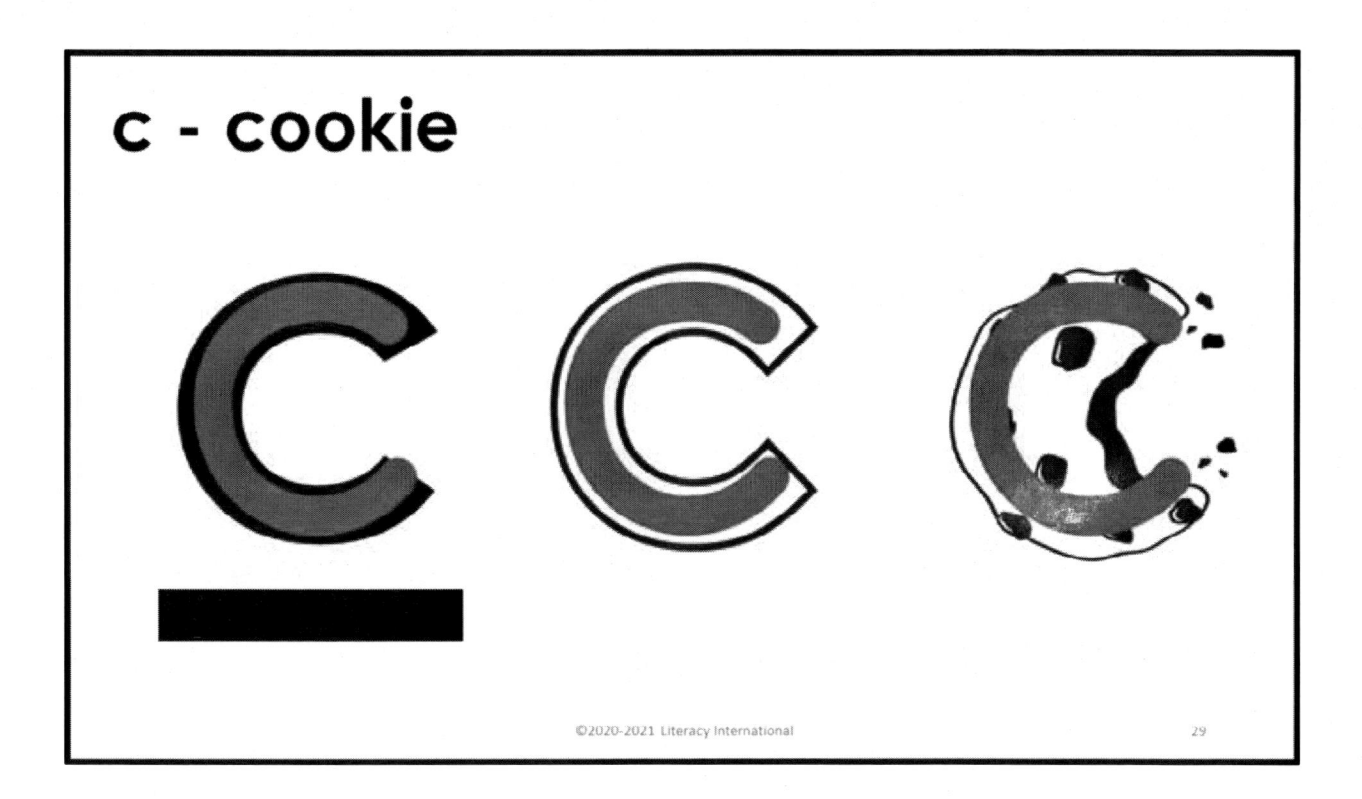

d - dog

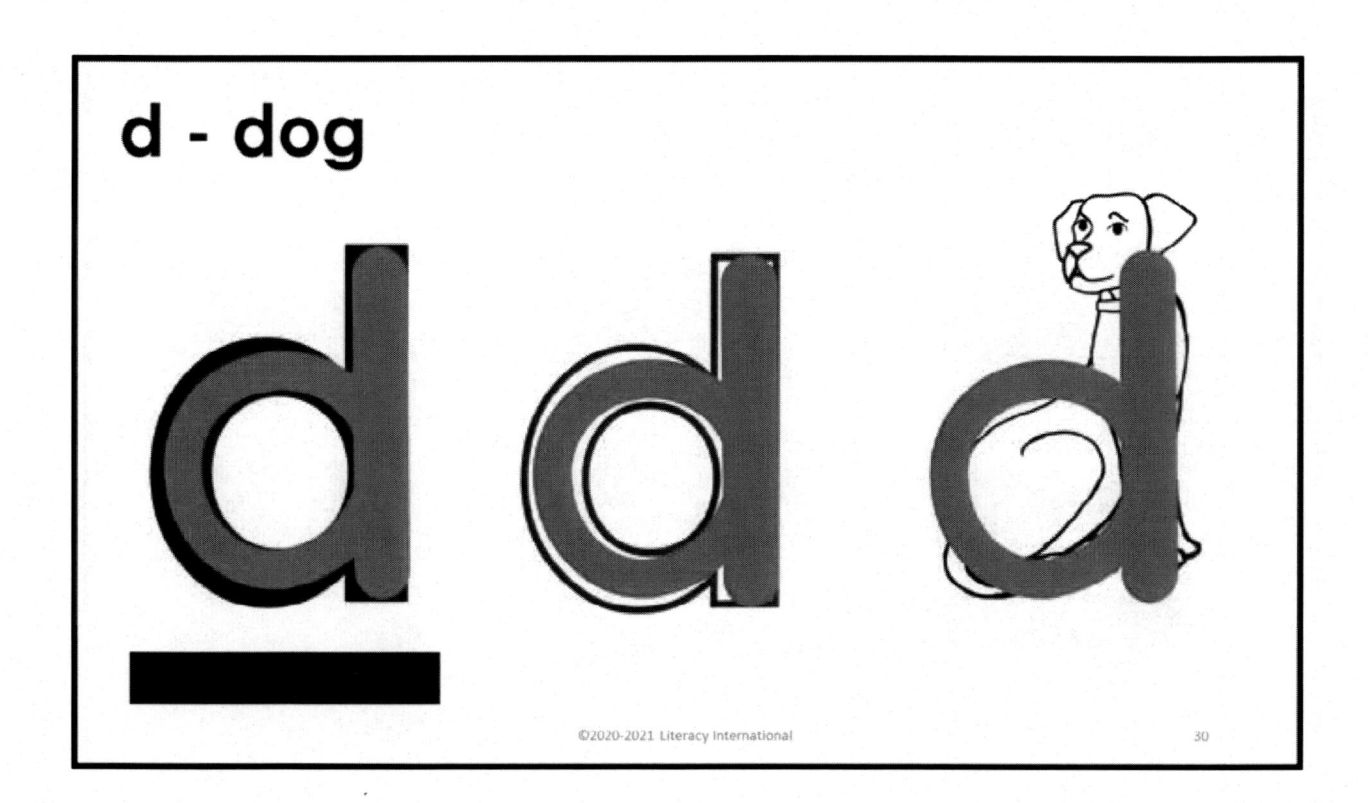

e - elf

f - frog

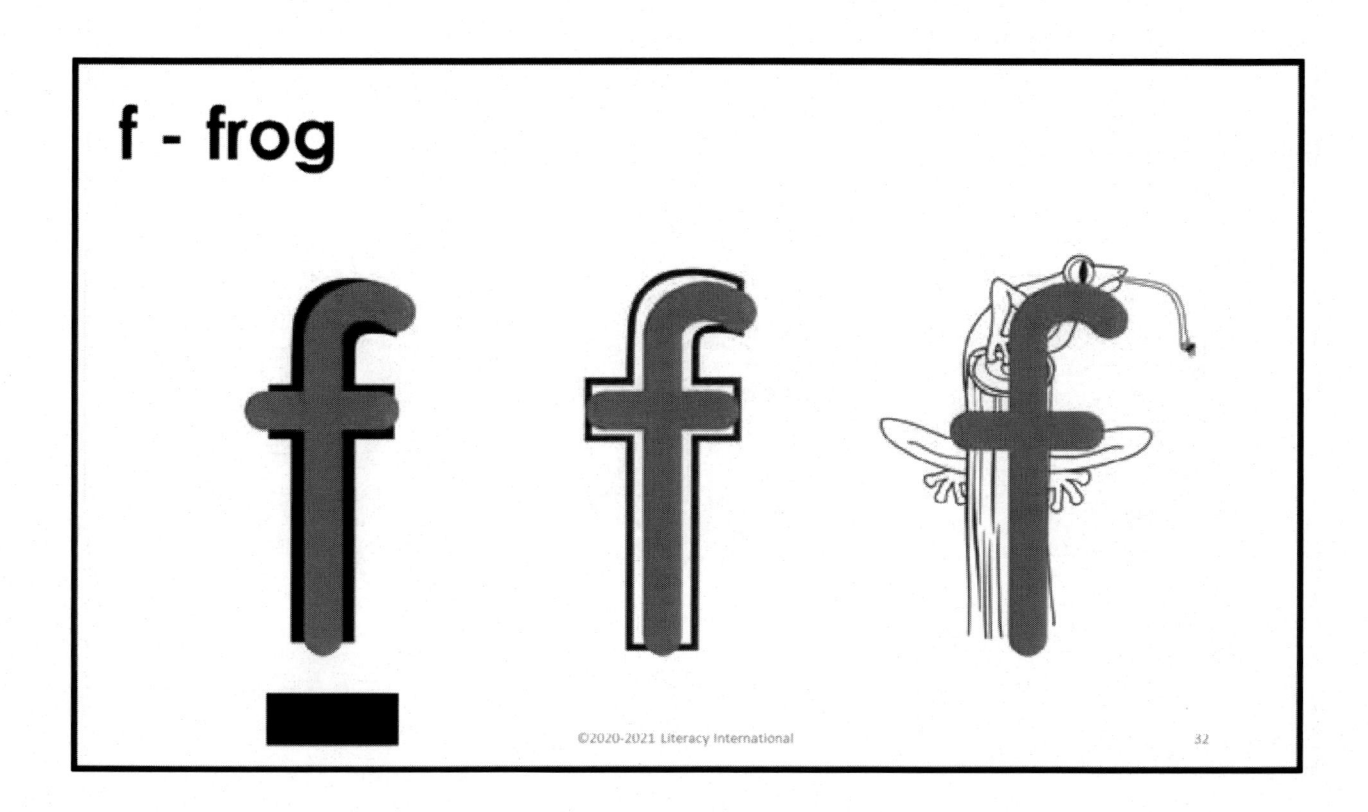

g - giggling girl

h - horse

i - itty bitty insect

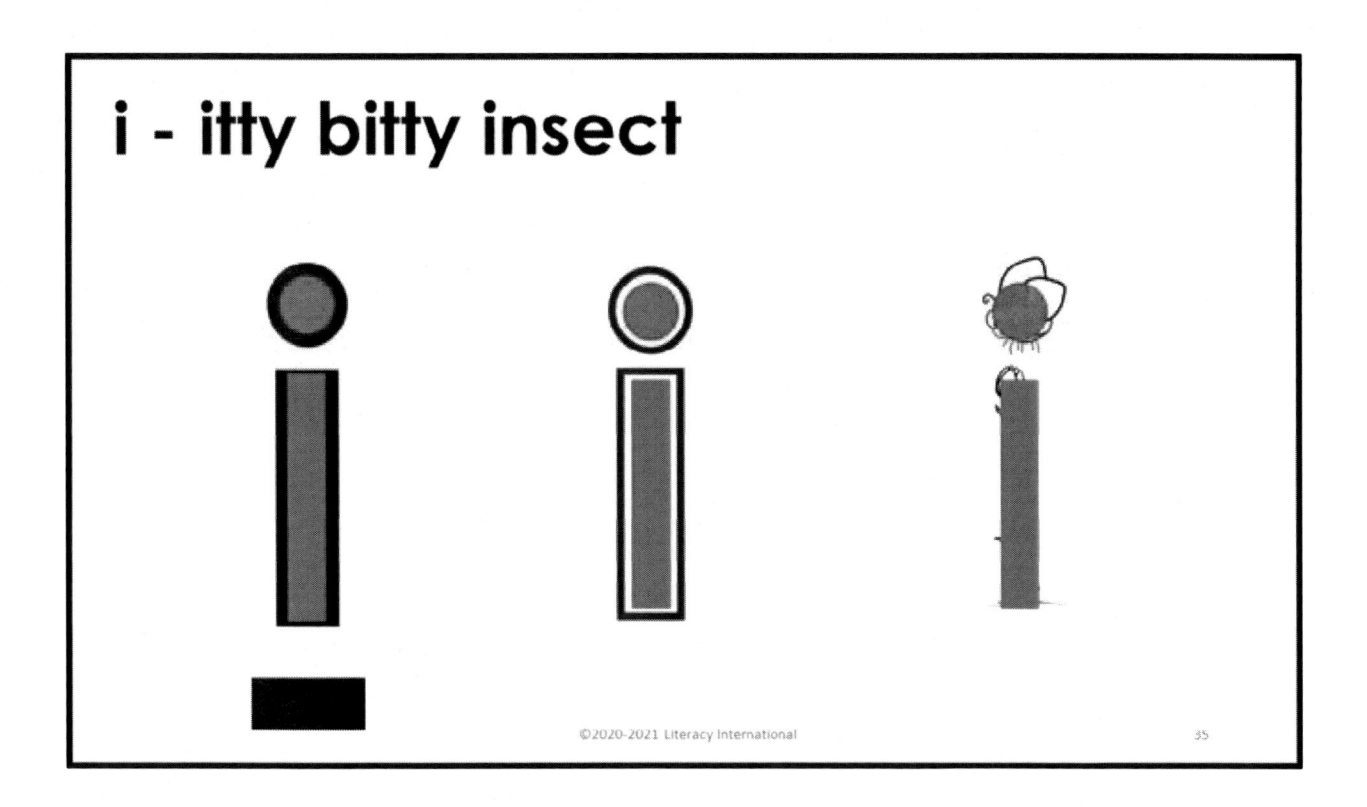

j - jumping Jill

k - kicking Kevin

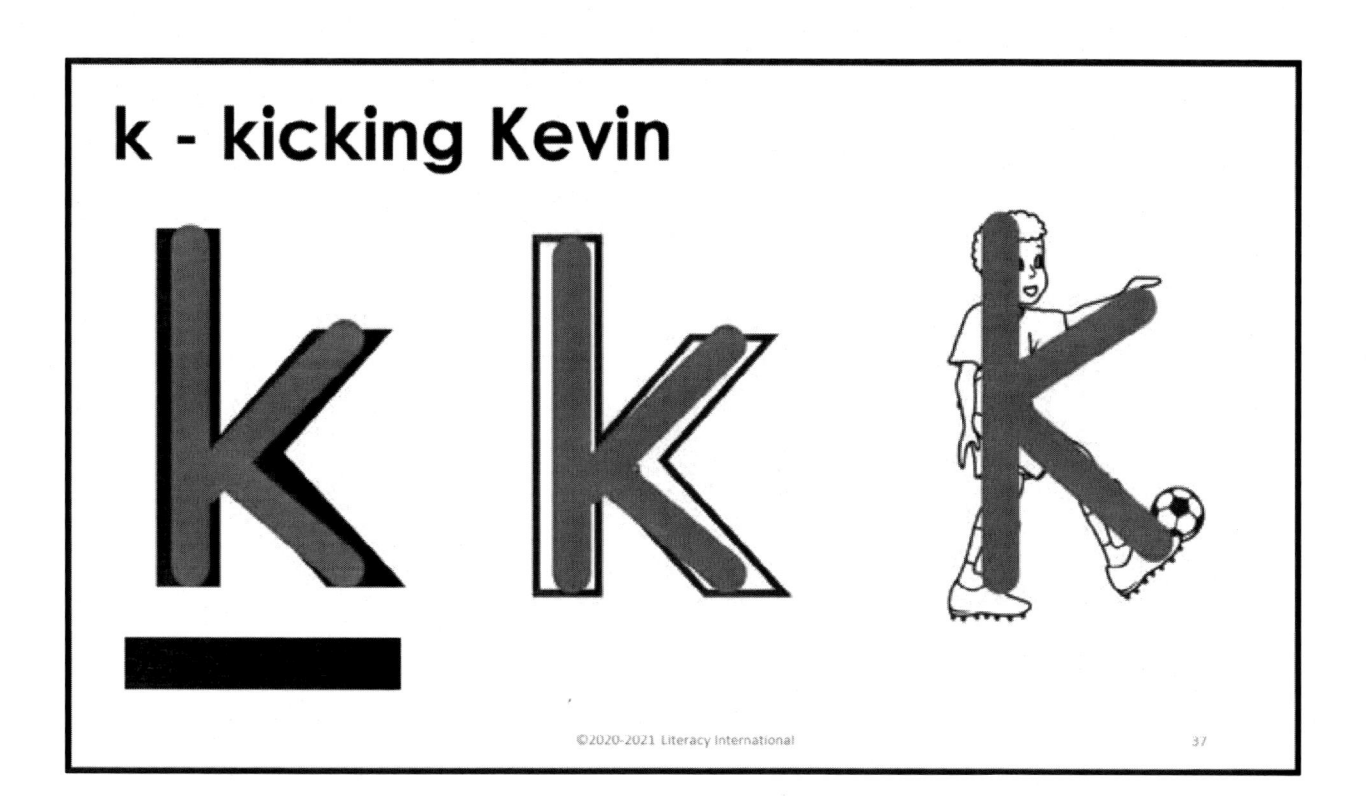

l - log

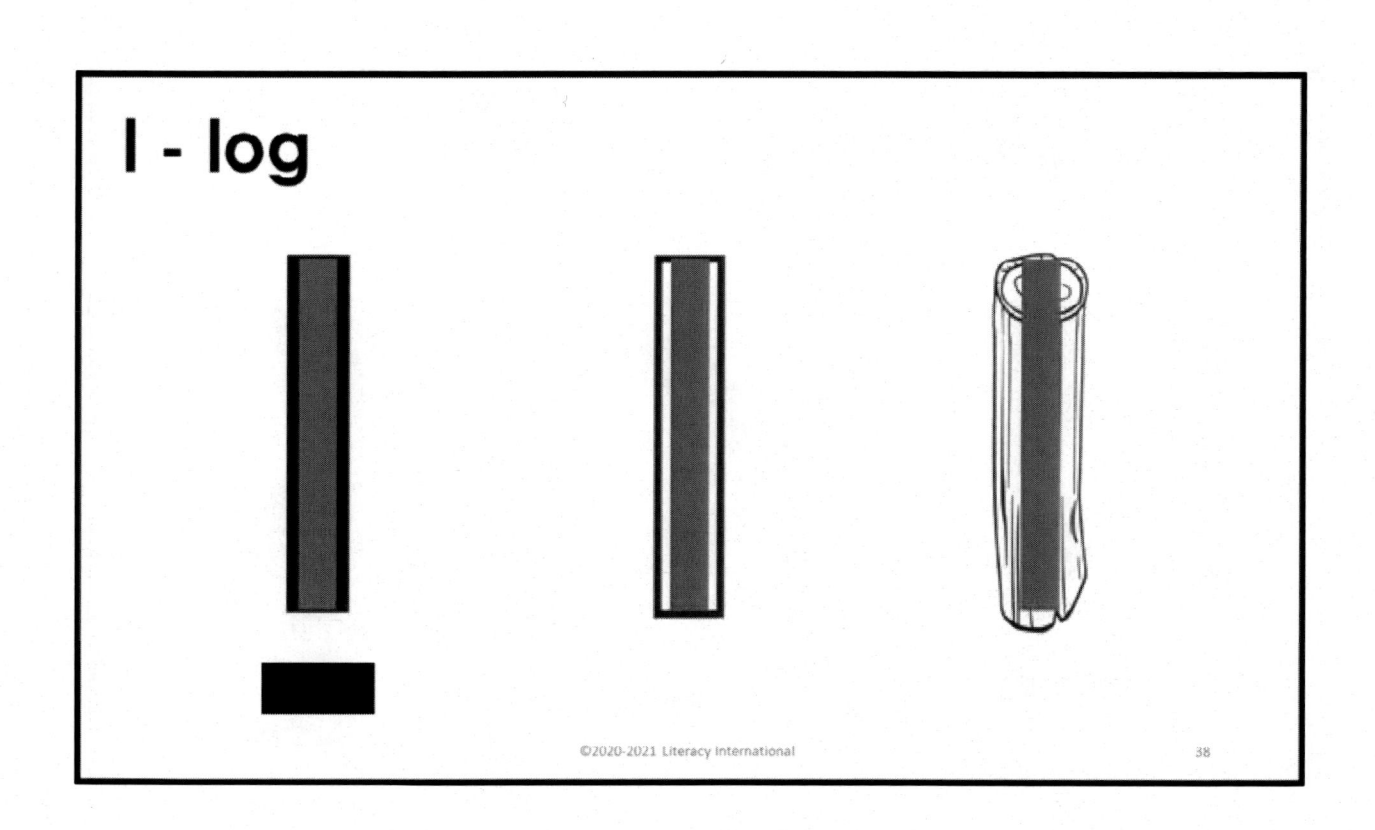

m - mountain

n - necklace

o - octopus

p - punch

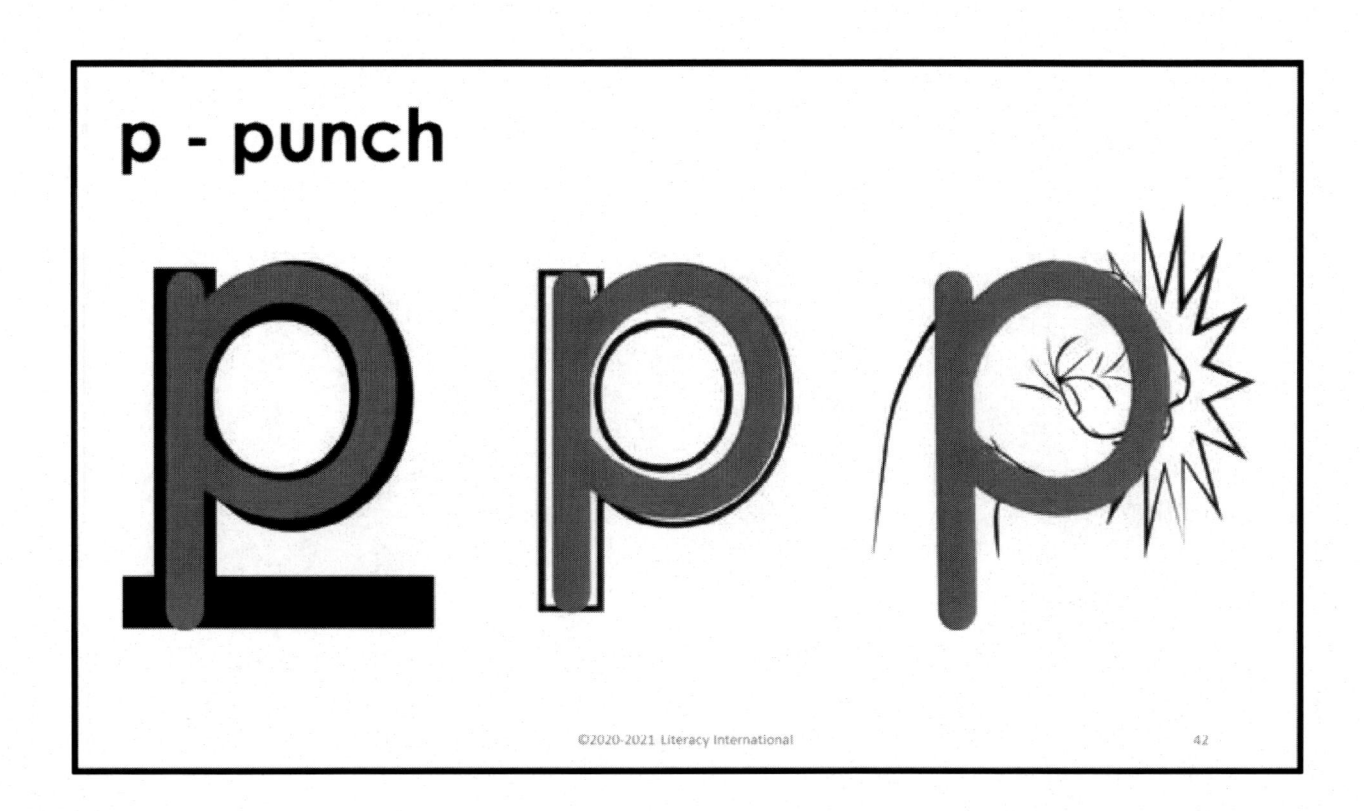

qu - quiet queen

r - rabbit

s - snake

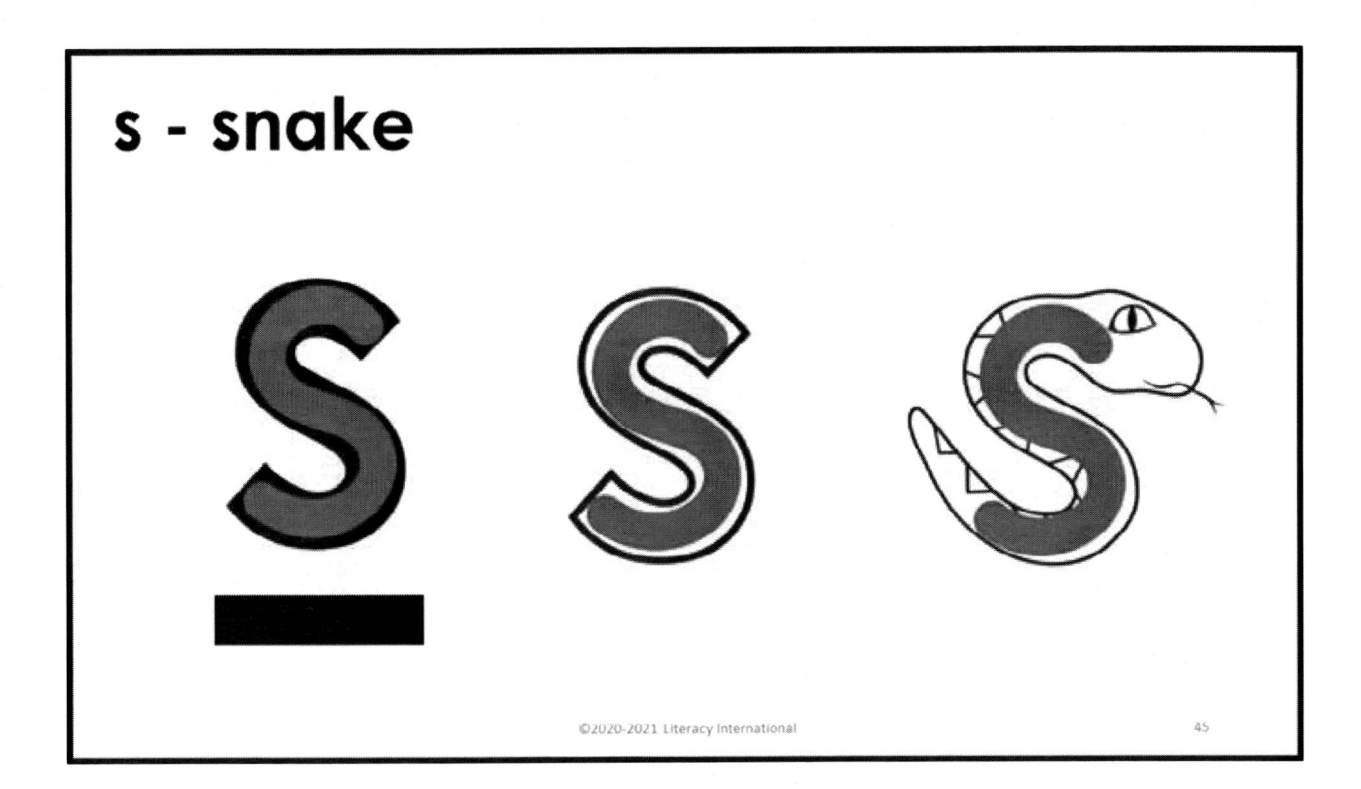

t - tools

u - up

v - volcano

w - waves

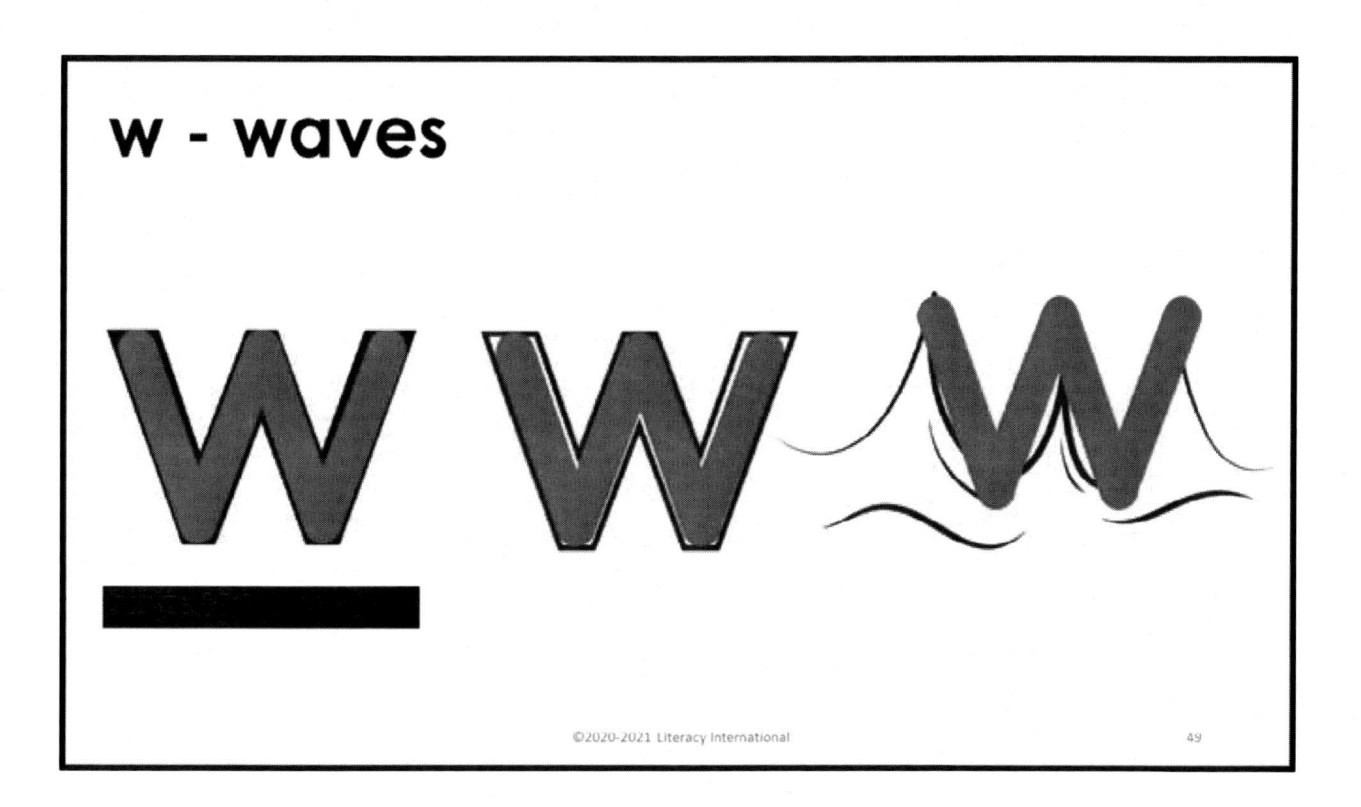

x - xbox

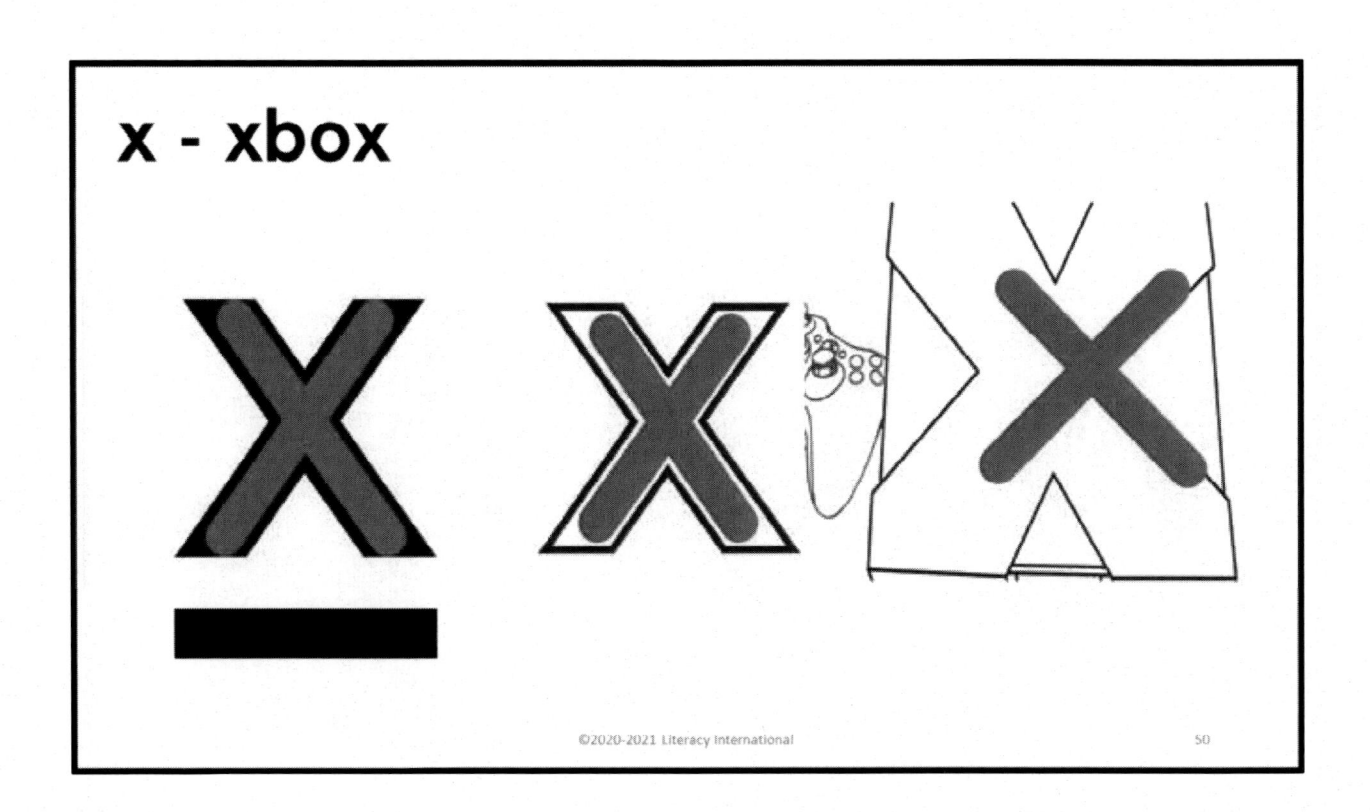

y - yoyo

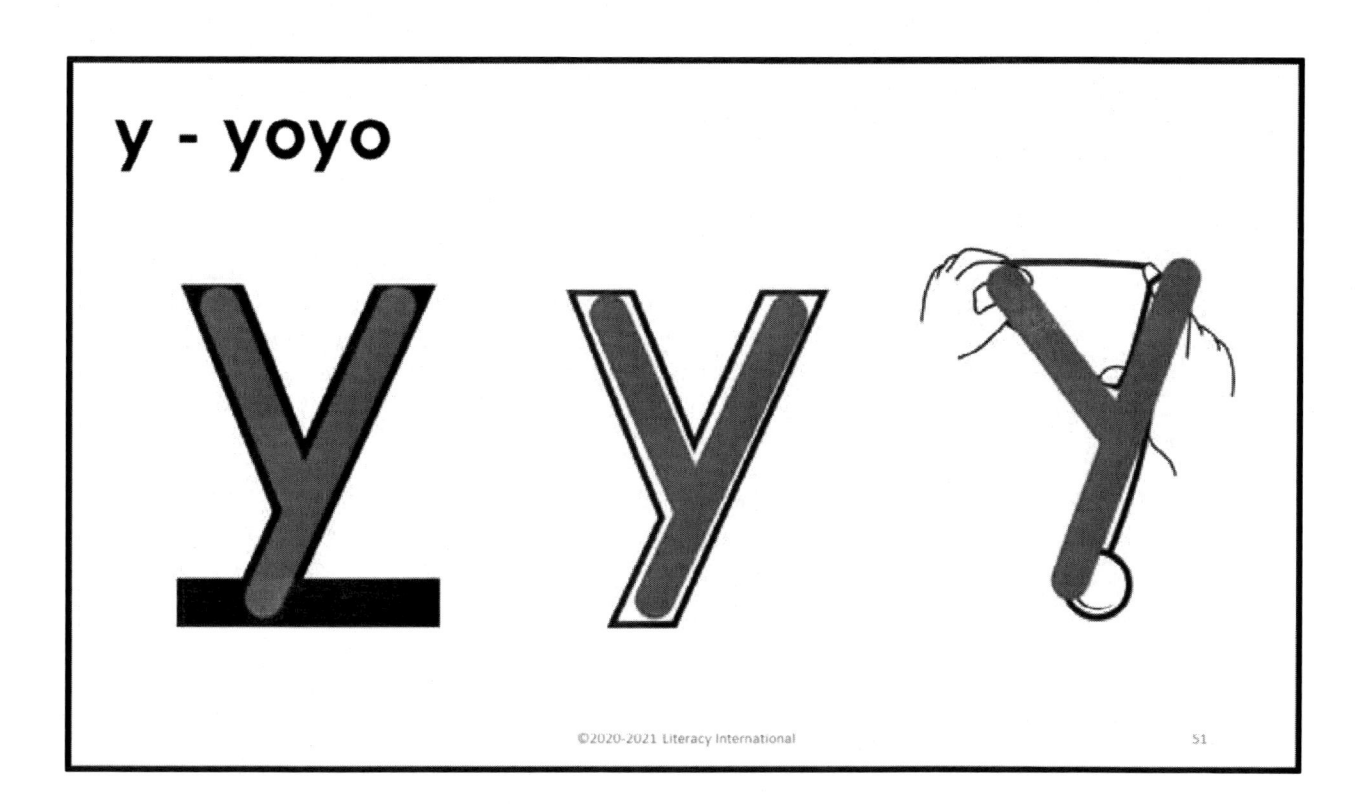

z - zebra

🔊 5. Homework – Circle the word (love)

Dear friends, we should love each other, because love comes from God. Everyone who loves has become God's child. And so everyone who (loves) knows God. Anyone who does not love does not know God, because God is love.

1 John 4:7-8 ERV

So we know the love that God has for us, and we trust that love.

God is love. Everyone who lives in love lives in God, and God lives in them.

1 John 4:16 ERV

Homework 5 – Bible Reading Review

Students may not understand all these words yet, but they can find and circle the word "love" and "loves" which appear several times in these verses from 1 John 4.

> ## 6. Homework – Choose 1 Verse to Memorize
>
> **A**
>
> God is love. Everyone who lives in love lives in God, and God lives in them.
>
> 1 John 4:16b ERV
>
> **B**
>
> I am the A and the Z, the first and the last, the beginning and the end.
>
> Revelation 22:13 GWT

Homework 6 – Memorize a Verse

Learners get to choose A, B, or C (on the next slide) to memorize. Please notice that the memory work is not long. Everyone, regardless of skill level, should be able to do it.

1. **Model.** Recite a verse from memory.

2. **Repeat.** Encourage students to find someone with whom to practice conversing and reading the completed homework assignment.

3. **Solo.** Students will recite the verse from memory at the next class.

Note for Revelation 22:13 - Many translations say "I am the Alpha and Omega," these are the first and last letters of the Greek alphabet. A and Z are the first and last letters of the English alphabet.

> ### 6. Homework – Choose 1 Verse to Memorize
>
> **C**
>
> Dear friends, we should love each other, because love comes from God. Everyone who loves has become God's child. And so everyone who loves knows God. Anyone who does not love does not know God, because God is love.
>
> 1 John 4:7-8 ERV

Homework – 6. Memorize a Verse

Learners get to choose A, B, (from previous slide) or C to memorize.

7. Count and write the numbers.

★ ★ ★ ★ ☐

▲▲▲▲▲▲▲ ☐

☁ ☁ ☁ ☁ ☁ ☁ ☐

📱 📱 📱 ☐

♥ ♥ ♥ ♥ ♥ ♥ ♥ ♥ ☐

7. Homework – vocabulary review

Count and write the numbers in the boxes.

8. Homework - Now I Can...

- ☐ I can spell and write my name.
- ☐ I can say and write my phone number.
- ☐ I can sing or say the ABC song.
- ☐ I can say and write the numbers 0-9
- ☐ I can say and write the letters A-Z.

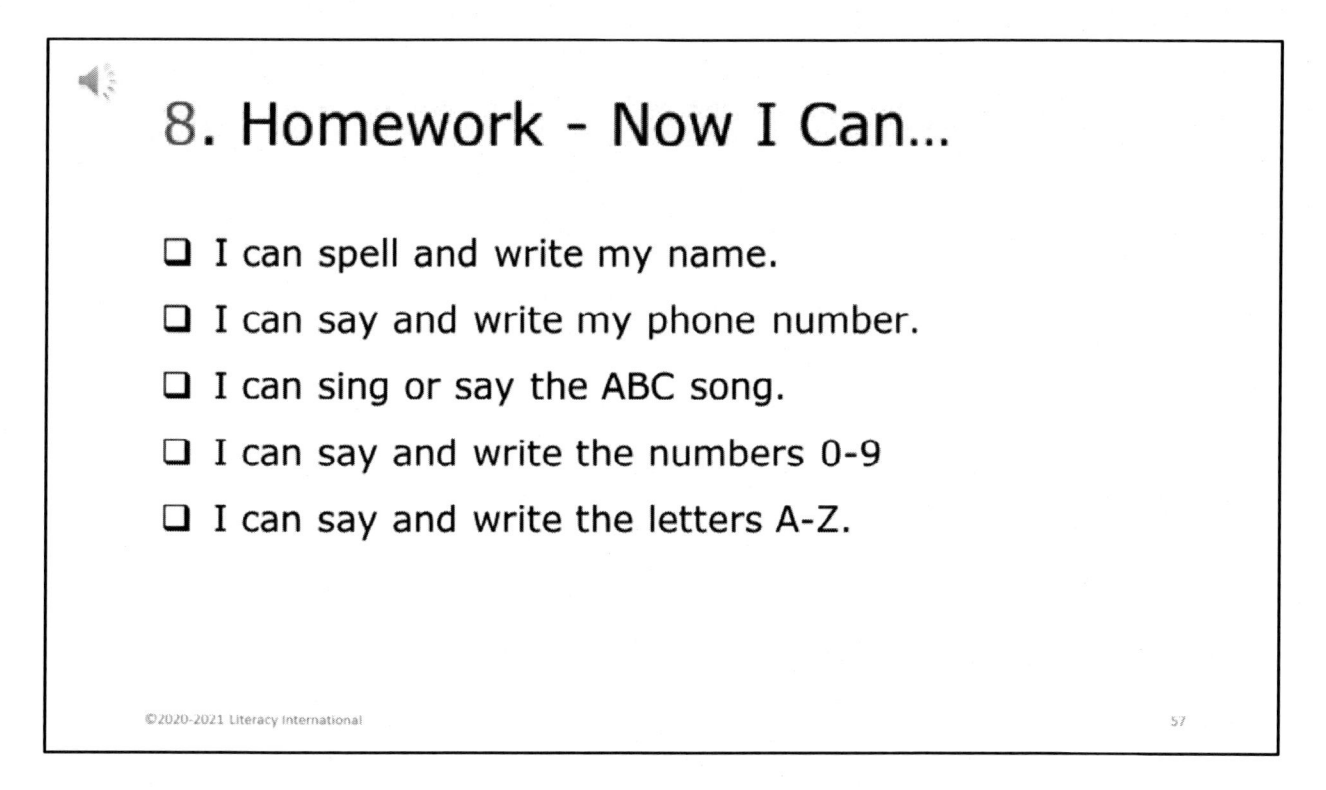

Homework 8 – I can statements

The student must be able to achieve all of these skills before the next lesson. If not, the lesson can be repeated or additional practice materials (see notes on slide 1) can be used.

Review all of the skills at the beginning of the next lesson. Be sure to give lots of praise and encouragement!

Closing Prayer

Pray

You may want to ask for any special prayer requests, then pray for your students and bless them.

Teacher's Notes:

Bible Reading: God loves you. – Isaiah 54:10, Luke 15:20
- **Theme:** Greetings
- **Pronunciation:** /a/ and /yU/
- **Grammar:**
- Hello my name is…
- What is your name?
- Nice to meet you.
- How are you?
- Fine, thank you.

Preparation:
- Pray
- Read Isaiah 54:10, Luke 15:20
- Preview slides and game
- Optional: Bring name tags or name cards for students and yourself.

> # Pray, Review, and Preview
>
> **Bible Reading:** God loves you. Isaiah 54:10, Luke 15:20
> **Theme:** Nice to meet you!
> **Pronunciation:** /a/ and /yU/
> **Grammar:**
> - Hello my name is...
> - What is your name?
> - Nice to meet you.
> - How are you?
> - Fine, thank you.

Pray

Pray for the class, thanking God for the people he puts in our lives to meet and for his love.

Check Homework and Review

Ask each student to read aloud or recite their homework from the last class. Check written work. Be sure they have read Isaiah 54:10 and Luke 15:20 in their native languages in preparation for the lesson. The hyperlink of the Bible verses will take you to https://live.bible.is/ where you can select from over 1,000 languages to read and listen to the verses.

Review the main points of the previous lesson, and ask if there are any questions.

What do you see?

Nice to meet you.
How are you?
I'm good!
Hello!

©2020-2021 Literacy International

1A. Discuss Theme Picture

- Ask "What do you see in this picture?" and "What else?" to elicit vocabulary they already know.
- Repeat and write their words or show the words on the next slide.
- Answers may include: people, wave, hug, handshake, etc.

More advanced students can be encouraged to make complete sentences:
"The men say hello. They shake hands."

What do you see?

shake hands   wave   hug   high five

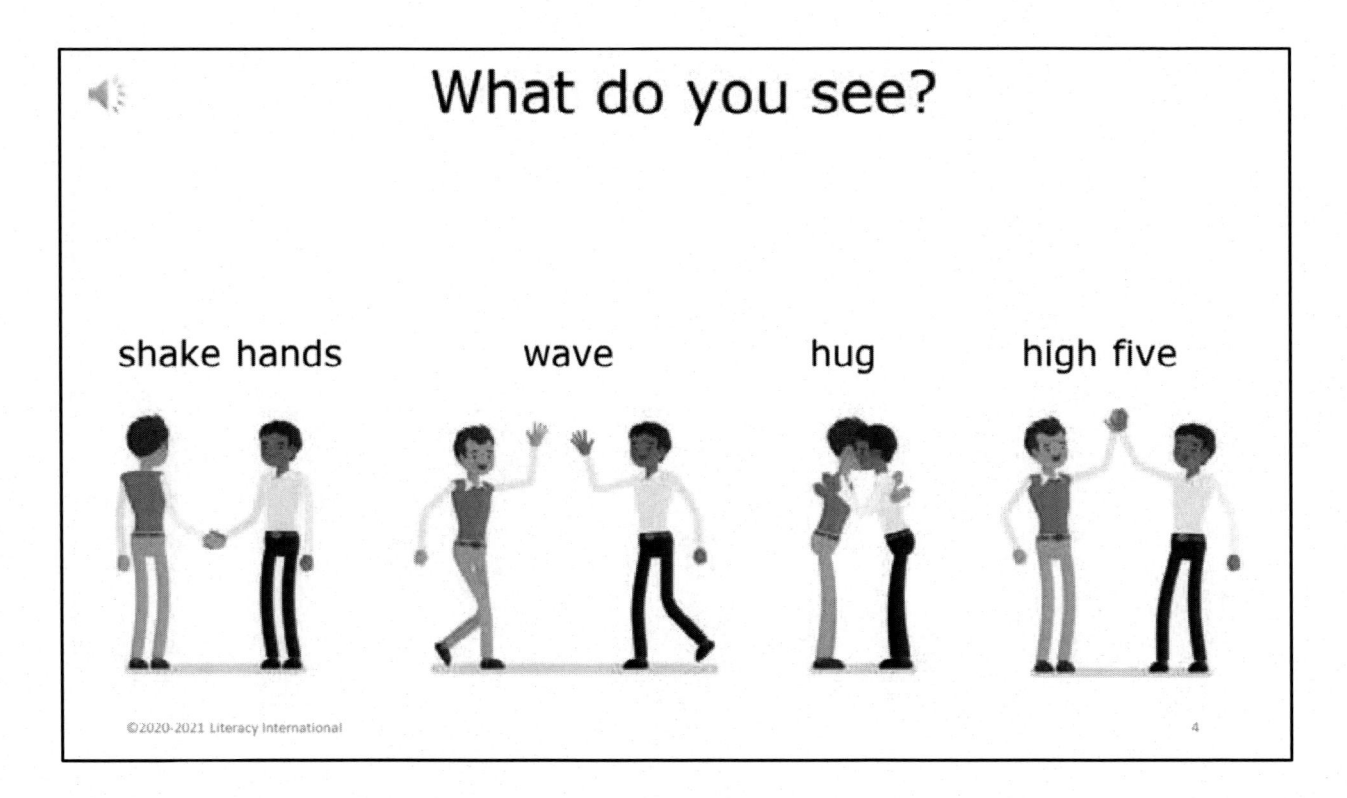

©2020-2021 Literacy International

1B. Show Words for the Theme Picture

Briefly show and demonstrate the words.

Listen and repeat.

1	2	3	4
a name	a hand	hello	goodbye
names	hands	I say hello.	They say goodbye.

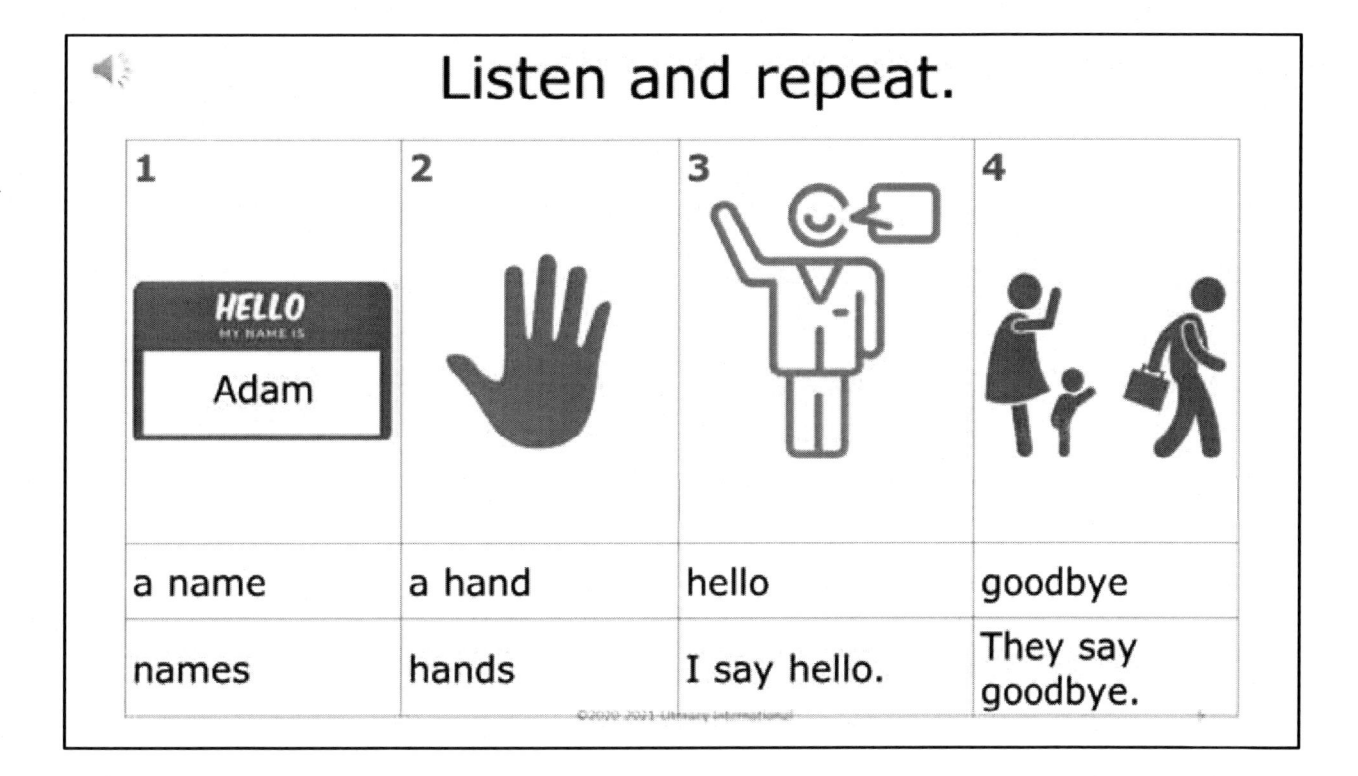

2A. Vocabulary

1. **Say the new words in a simple sentence:** "This is a name" several times, while indicating the picture or your own name tag. Students just watch and listen. Be sure to use a natural speaking voice and good rhythm and intonation.

2. **Say the word and the article that goes with it several times**, as you indicate the object. For example, say: *a name, a name, a name*. Have your students then repeat the word after you several times.

3. **Say the word in the same sentence again.** Have students repeat after you each time, "This is a name."

4. **Check students' comprehension by asking direct questions.** For example, *What is this? (a name). Is this a hand?*

02-5

Listen and repeat.

5	6	7	8
bad	good	to meet	to hug
This is bad.	This is good.	Nice to meet you.	We hug.

2B. Vocabulary

1. **Say the new words in a simple sentence:** "This is bad" several times, while indicating the object or picture. Students just watch and listen. Be sure to use a natural speaking voice and good rhythm and intonation.

2. **Say the word and the article that goes with it several times**, as you indicate the object. For example, say: *bad, bad, bad*. Have your students then repeat the word after you several times.

3. **Say the word in the same sentence again**. Have students repeat after you each time, "This is bad."

4. **Check students' comprehension by asking direct questions**. For example, *What is bad? Is this good?*

Listen and repeat.

9	10	11	12
to wave	to shake hands	to love	to smile
Wave hello!	We shake hands.	God loves you.	I smile.

2C. Vocabulary

1. **Say the new words in a simple sentence:** "Wave hello" several times, while indicating the object or picture. Students just watch and listen. Be sure to use a natural speaking voice and good rhythm and intonation.

2. **Say the word and the preposition that goes with it several times**, as you indicate the object. For example, say: *to wave, to wave, to wave*. Have your students then repeat the word after you several times.

3. **Say the word in the same sentence again**. Have students repeat after you each time, "Wave hello."

4. **Check students' comprehension by asking direct questions**. For example, *What is this? Is this to wave?"*

Listen and repeat.

	Phrase	Response
1.	Hello, how are you?	I'm good, thanks. I'm fine, thank you.
2.	Nice to meet you!	Nice to meet you, too.
3.	Hi, my name is ____.	Hi, my name is ____.
4.	What is your name?	My name is ____.
5.	Goodbye.	Goodbye.

2D. Grammar – Simple greetings and phrases.

Model, Repeat, and Solo the pronunciation of all phrases shown on the chart.

You can explain that in informal speech people say "hi" and "I'm good," while in formal speech they say "hello" and "I am fine." Both are acceptable.

> # Listen and repeat.
>
> A: Hi, how are you?
> B: I'm good, thanks. And you?
> A: I'm good.
>
>
> A: Hello, how are you?
> B: I am fine, thank you. And you?
> A: I'm fine.
>
> ©2020-2021 Literacy International

3. Conversation

These two conversations demonstrate the formal and informal greetings. You may also practice shaking hands and waving.

1. **Model: Say both parts of the conversation several times.** Use A and B cards, stick figures, or change your physical position to indicate the dual parts. Role play the parts to convey the meaning of the conversation. **Students are to watch and listen.**

2. **Repeat: Say one line at a time, and have students repeat until they can be understood.**

3. **Solo: You begin the conversation and call on individual students to respond.** Then reverse the roles (students are A, you are B).

4. Once students can do both parts, **encourage free conversation.**

> ## Listen and repeat.
>
> A: Hi, my name is Paul. What is your name?
> B: I am John.
> A: Nice to meet you, John!
> B. Nice to meet you, too.
> A. I need to go to class now. Goodbye!
> B. Goodbye.

3. Conversation 2

You may also practice shaking hands and waving.

1. **Model: Say both parts of the conversation several times.** Use A and B cards, stick figures, or change your physical position to indicate the dual parts. Role-play the parts to convey the meaning of the conversation. **Students are to watch and listen.**

2. **Repeat: Say one line at a time, and have students repeat until they can be understood.**

3. **Solo: You begin the conversation and call on individual students to respond.** First you will take the A part, then you will reverse the roles (students are A, you are B).

4. Once students can do both parts, **encourage free conversation**, substituting their own words for the blue words.

Listen and repeat.

1. /a/	2. /yU/	3. Challenge
am	you	
bad	use	
man	computer	
hand	music	

1. You use a computer for music.
2. I am a man.

---

4. Pronunciation- Sound and Spelling

1. **Model: Say the sound several times while pointing to it.** (For example, point to the **a** and say /a/ /a/ /a/. **Then say the sound and quickly read the entire list, pointing to each item as you read it** (/a/ am, bad, man, hand). Students just watch and listen.

2. **Repeat: Say the sound and each word several times, having students repeat each time after you in unison.** Be sure to use your normal voice and rate of speed. Do one column at a time, top to bottom.

3. **Solo: Call on individuals to say a sound and its word group.** Give lots of praise.

4. **Challenge:** Choose another sound from the lesson that is challenging for your particular students to pronounce. Use words

02-11a

from Parts 1 and 2 of the lesson and from previous lessons to make a group of 3-5 words. You may repeat the same challenging sounds in several lessons. Students need a lot of practice on sounds that do not exist in their first language.

5. Read the sentences.

Listen and repeat.

—	—	—
	-	-
wave	listen	goodbye
you	seven	hello
meet	English	to meet
love	thank you	repeat

4. Hum and clap the stress.

Begin by humming the stress of a column of words. Hum higher, longer, and louder for big dashes, lower, shorter and quieter for small dashes.

You may use hand gestures to indicate that **the stressed syllable is higher in pitch, longer in duration, and louder.** Invite your students to join in humming the rhythm. Once the class is humming the rhythm in unison, you can begin saying the words. You may also wish to clap the syllables while you say the words.

1. Model: Hum and then say each word in the group several times. Students listen.
2. Repeat: students repeat words after you in unison.
3. Solo: call on individuals to read the entire group of words.

> **God loves you.**
> Luke 15:20 ERV
>
> While the son was still a long way off, his father saw him coming and felt sorry for him. So he ran to him and hugged and kissed him.

5A. Bible Reading:

Students have already read this verse in their native language as part of their homework, so it will be familiar even if they do not know all the vocabulary yet. The hyperlink of the Bible verses will take you to https://live.bible.is/ where you can select from over 1,000 languages to read and listen to the verses and watch the video. The pictures also help them to understand.

A. Ask students to read the verse again in their language.
B. Read the story out loud to the class in English.
C. **Act out the story,** using gestures to express **saw, ran, hugged** and **kissed.**
D. Write words that students ask about and give simple definitions.
E. Ask if there are any questions or comments about the verse.

> **God loves you.**
> Isaiah 54:10 ERV
>
> "The mountains may disappear, and the hills may become dust, but my faithful love will never leave you. I will make peace with you and it will never end." The Lord who loves you said this.

5B. Bible Reading:

Students have already read this verse in their native language as part of their homework, so it will be familiar even if they do not know all the vocabulary yet. The hyperlink of the Bible verses will take you to https://live.bible.is/ where you can select from over 1,000 languages to read and listen to the verses. The pictures also help them to understand.

A. Ask students to read the verse again in their language.
B. Read the verse out loud to the class in English.
C. Write words that students ask about and give simple definitions.
D. Ask if there are any questions or comments about the verse.

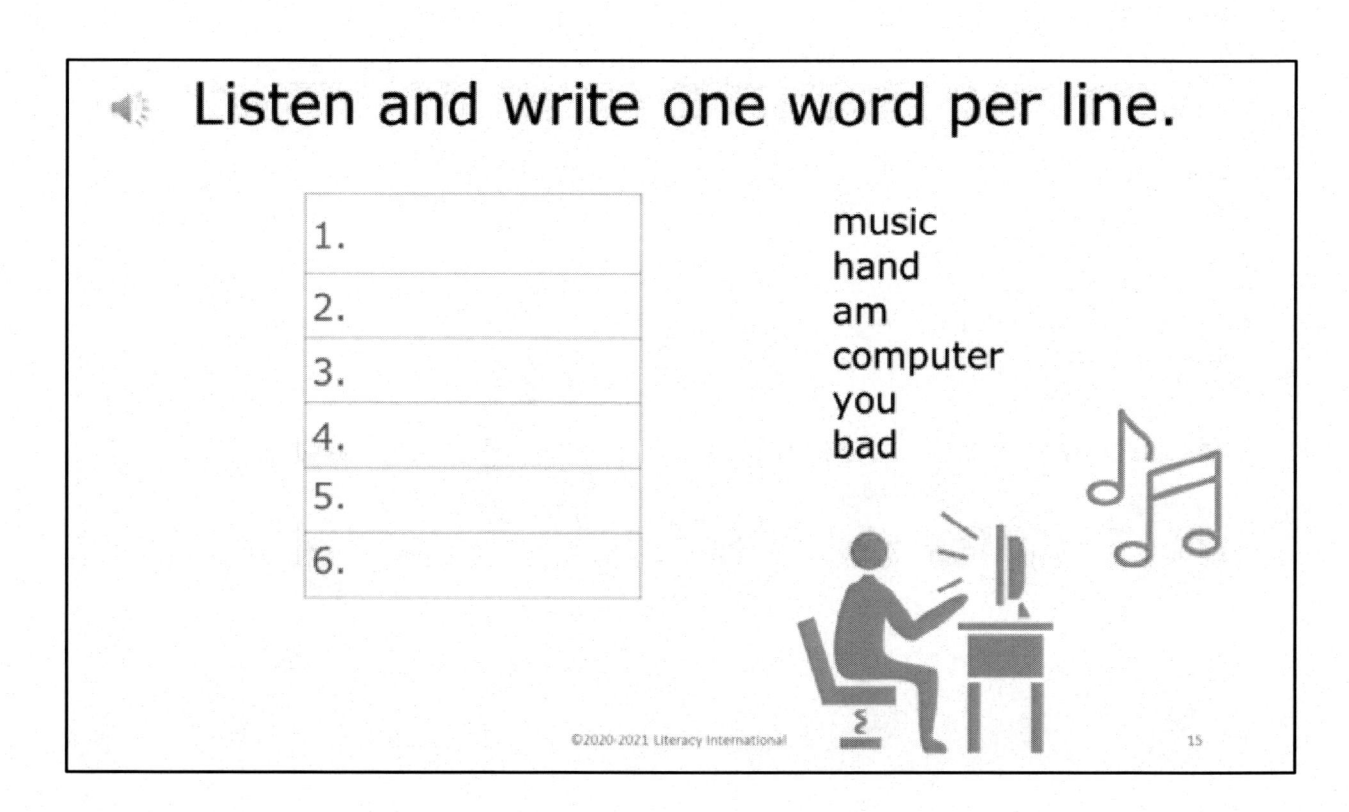

> **Listen and write one word per line.**
>
> 1.
> 2.
> 3.
> 4.
> 5.
> 6.
>
> music
> hand
> am
> computer
> you
> bad

6A. Activities - Dictation of sound/spelling words

Read the words with a sample sentence and have students write just one word for each line. Check spelling.

For more advanced students, you can hide the sample word bank.

1. am, am (I am fine.) am.
2. you, you, (God loves you.) you
3. music, music (The music is good.) music
4. computer, computer (I use a computer.) computer
5. bad, bad, (This is bad.) bad
6. hand, hand, (Wave your hand.) hand

Ask your partner.

Questions	Answers
1. How are you?	
2. What is your name?	
3. How do you spell your name?	
4. What is your phone number?	

6B. Activities - Pair work

Ask students to interview a partner and write their partner's answers. Then they will switch roles and answer their partner's questions.
Check answers for correct grammar, spelling, and punctuation.

Fill in the words and practice.

6C. Activities - Pair work

Students fill in the speech bubbles with what the people say. Check answers for correct grammar, spelling, and punctuation. Answers will vary.

Give an example, "Hello, I'm Joe." "Nice, to meet you. I'm Sue."

Then partners act out the 3 conversations.

Game - Charades

Act out the vocabulary words.

7. Game
Charades: Each student takes turns acting out various vocabulary words. The person who guesses the most correctly is the winner.

1. Model: Act out each of the vocabulary words: **wave, smile, love, good, bad,** etc. and have the students guess the word.

2. Repeat: have the students do the acting out gestures with you.

3. Solo: Have the students act out the words and guess what the words are.

> ## 1 & 2 Homework
>
> 1. Read the next lesson's Bible verses: Matthew 6:9 and John 4:14 in your language.
>
> 2. Fill in the words. Letter A is an example.
>
> A. Hello, how are **you**?
> B. ___ fine, thank you.
> C. Nice to ___ you.
> D. ___ to meet you, too.
> E. What is your phone ___?
> F. What is your ___?
> G. God ___ you.
>
> | loves |
> | name |
> | meet |
> | I'm |
> | **you** |
> | number |
> | nice |
>
> ©2020-2021 Literacy International
>
> 19

Homework 1 and 2 - Reading the next Bible Lesson in L1, and writing new vocabulary

Students will always read the Bible lesson in their first language (L1) before reading it in English the following lesson. Help them get a Bible in their own language. The hyperlink of the Bible verses will take you to https://live.bible.is/ where you can select from over 1,000 languages to read and listen to the verses and watch the video.

Model. Go over each of the **homework assignments** to be sure the students understand what to do.
Repeat. Encourage students to find someone with whom to practice conversing and reading the completed homework assignment. They may use a bilingual dictionary.
Solo. Students will share their homework when they are finished. Be sure to check it for correctness, including spelling. Explain mistakes, and give praise and encouragement.
    Answers #2:
    B. I'm fine, thank you.

C. Nice to meet you.
D. Nice to meet you, too.
E. What is your phone number?
F. What is your name?
G. God loves you.

3. Write the words

1 ✋	2	3	4 HELLO Adam	5	6 ☺
a hand					
hands					

7 🤝	8 👎	9 👍	10 ♡♡	11	12

Homework 3 – Write the vocabulary words with the pictures

This homework practices writing the new vocabulary words in singular and plural forms as well as the verbs in sentence form.

Answers: Number 1 is an example.
1. a hand, hands
2. hello, I say hello.
3. goodbye, They say goodbye.
4. a name, names
5. to meet, Nice to meet you.
6. a smile, smiles
7. to shake hands, We shake hands.
8. bad, This is bad.
9. good, This is good.
10. to love, God loves you.
11. to hug. We hug.
12. to wave. Wave hello.

02-20

4. Write and say the words

A. I am Adam. Nice to meet you.	
B. The man shakes hands.	
C. This is bad.	
D. You use the computer.	
E. God loves you.	
F. The music is good!	

Homework 4 – Write and say sentences with the new sounds.

This homework practices writing, spelling and pronouncing the **/a/** and **/yU/** sounds.

5. **Write the Bible verses from the lesson.**

Isaiah 54:10, ERV

_____

_____

_____

Luke 15:20, ERV

_____

_____

_____

Homework 5 – Writing practice. Write the Bible verses from the lesson.

Students may look back at the verses to copy them here.

> ### 🔊 6. Homework – Choose 1 Verse to Memorize
>
> **A**
>
> "The mountains may disappear, and the hills may become dust, but my faithful love will never leave you. I will make peace with you and it will never end." The Lord who loves you said this.
> Isaiah 54:10, ERV
>
> **B**
>
> While the son was still a long way off, his father saw him coming and felt sorry for him. So he ran to him and hugged and kissed him. Luke 15:20, ERV

Homework 6 – Memorize a Verse

Learners get to choose A or B to memorize. Please notice that the memory work is not long. Everyone, regardless of skill level, should be able to do it.

1. Model. Recite a verse from memory.

2. Repeat. Encourage students to find someone with whom to practice conversing and reading the completed homework assignment.

3. Solo. Students will recite the verse from memory at the next class.

> # 7. Homework - Now I Can...
>
> - ☐ I can say hello, goodbye and nice to meet you.
> - ☐ I can ask "How are you?" and answer "I am good/fine."
> - ☐ I can read, write, say, and understand the 12 vocabulary words.
> - ☐ I understand that God loves me.

Homework 7 – I can statements

The student must be able to achieve all of these skills before the next lesson. If not, the lesson can be repeated.
Review all of the skills at the beginning of the next lesson. Be sure to give lots of praise and encouragement!

Closing Prayer

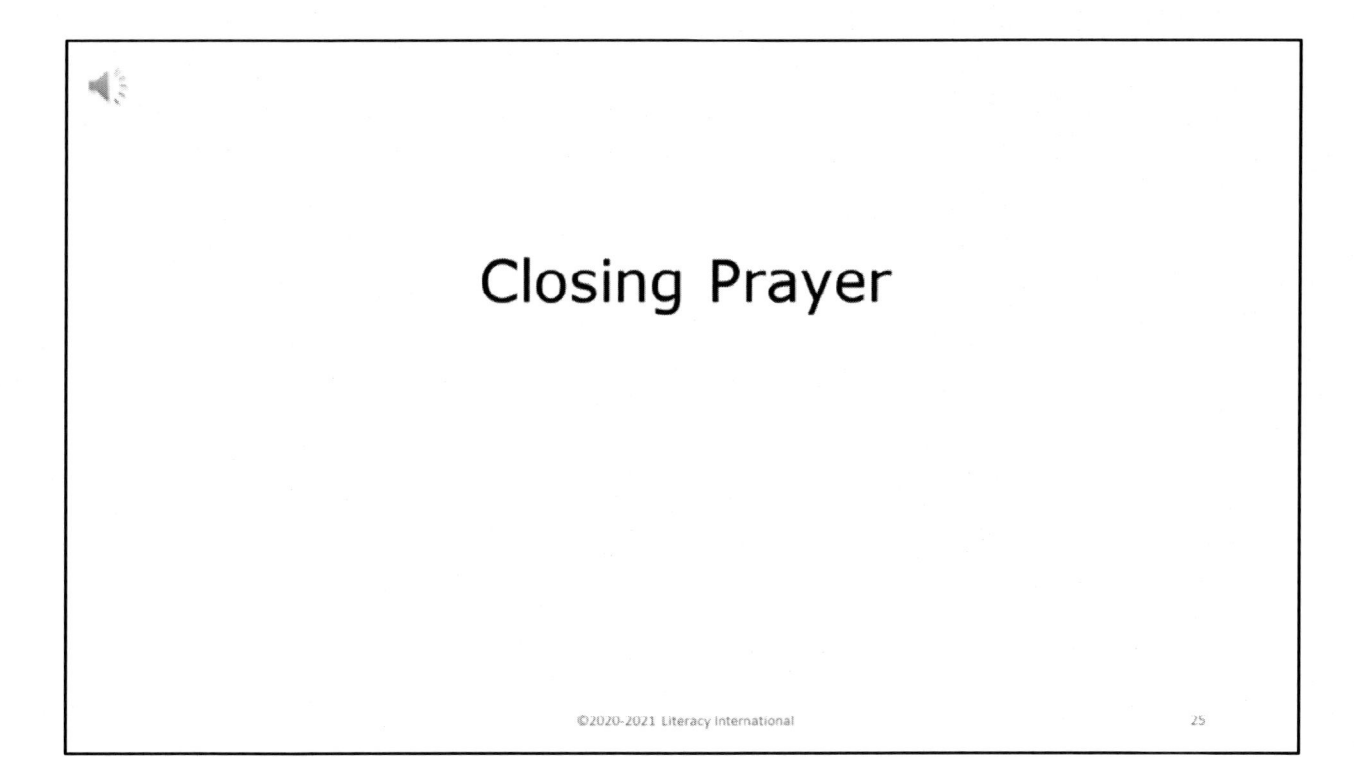

Pray
You may want to ask for any special prayer requests, then pray for your students and bless them.

Light of the WORLD
Learning English through the Bible
Lesson A1-03
©2020-2021 Literacy International

Teacher's Notes:
Bible Reading: God is our father - Matthew 6:9, John 4:14
Theme: Basic needs
Pronunciation: /A/ and /b/
Grammar: I need...
Preparation:
- Pray
- Read Matthew 6:9, John 4:14
- Preview slides and song
- Optional: Bring bottled water, food, forks, spoons. Preview videos of the Bible verses (if you wish to show them) at https://live.bible.is/

> ## Pray, Review, and Preview
>
> **Bible Reading:** God is our Father - Matthew 6:9, John 4:14
> **Theme:** Basic needs
> **Pronunciation:** /A/ and /b/
> **Grammar:** I need…
>
> ©2020-2021 Literacy International

Pray
Pray for the class. You may want to thank the Lord for being our Father.

Check Homework and Review

Ask students to read aloud or recite their homework from the last class. Check written work. Be sure they have read Matthew 6:9 and John 4:14 in their native languages in preparation for the lesson. The hyperlinks of the Bible verses will take you to https://live.bible.is/ where you can select from over 1,000 languages to read and listen to the verses and watch the videos, if you wish.

Review the main points of the previous lesson and ask if there are any questions.

What do you see?

1A. Discuss Theme Picture

- Ask "What do you see in this picture?" and "What else?" to elicit vocabulary they already know.
- Repeat and write their words or show the words on the next slide.

Answers may include: bottle, water, drink, eat, fork, spoon, plate, glass, cup, table, chair, people, food, etc.

More advanced students can be encouraged to make complete sentences:
They eat at the table.

What do you see?

1. spoon
2. fork
3. table
4. bottle
5. water
6. food

1B. Show Words for Theme Picture

Please show the names of the theme picture items to the students briefly.
These words can be studied for homework.
Practice of vocabulary begins with the following slide.

Listen and repeat.

1	2	3	4
water*	to help	food*	a table
	Please help.		tables

2A. Vocabulary

*Note: Food and Water and Bread are non-count nouns and are not usually used in the plural form. They are used with a singular verb and preceded by "some" instead of "a" in the indefinite form. They are often used with containers or measurements: Two bottles of water, Three plates of food, etc.

1. **Say the new words in a simple sentence: "This is water."** several times, while indicating the object or picture. Students just watch and listen. Be sure to use a natural speaking voice, and good rhythm and intonation.

2. **Say the word and the article that goes with it several times**, as you indicate the object. For example, say: *water, water, water*. Have your students then repeat the word after you several times.

03-5a

3. **Say the word in the same sentence again.** Have students repeat after you each time, "This is water."

4. **Check students' comprehension by asking direct questions.** For example, *What is this? Where's the food? Is this a table?*

Listen and repeat.

5	6	7	8
to drink	to eat	a spoon	a fork
I drink water.	We eat food.	spoons	forks

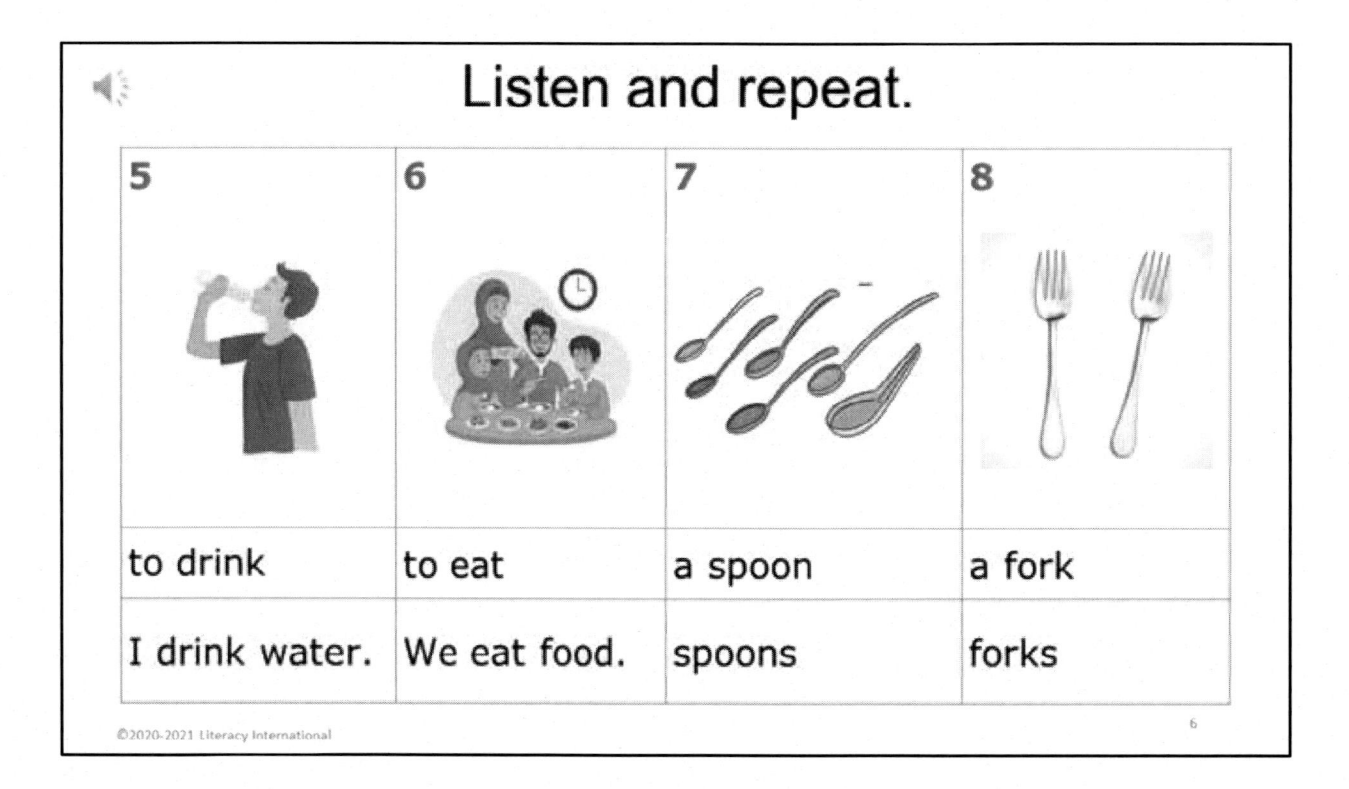

©2020-2021 Literacy International

2B. Vocabulary

1. **Say the new words in a simple sentence: "This is a fork."** several times, while indicating the object or picture. Students just watch and listen. Be sure to use a natural speaking voice, and good rhythm and intonation.

2. **Say the word and the article that goes with it several times**, as you indicate the object. For example, say: *a fork, a fork, a fork*. Have your students then repeat the word after you several times.

3. **Say the word in the same sentence again**. Have students repeat after you each time, "This is a fork."

4. **Check students' comprehension by asking direct questions**. For example, *What is this? Where's the spoon? Is this to drink?*

03-6

Listen and repeat.

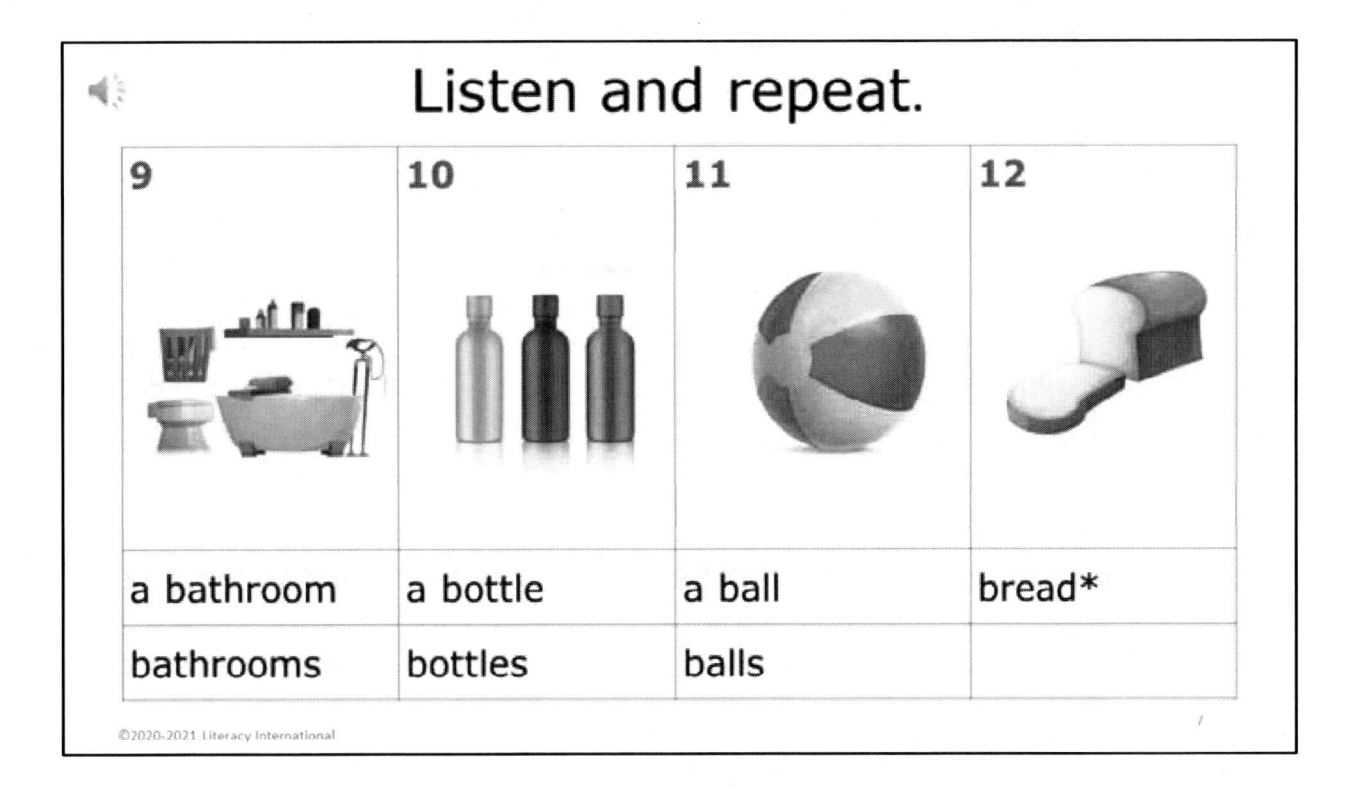

9	10	11	12
a bathroom	a bottle	a ball	bread*
bathrooms	bottles	balls	

2C. Vocabulary

*Note: Food and Water and Bread are non-count nouns and are not usually used in the plural form. They are used with a singular verb and preceded by "some" instead of "a" in the indefinite form. They are often used with containers or measurements: Four loaves of bread, etc.

1. **Say the new words in a simple sentence: "This is a bathroom."** several times, while indicating the object or picture. Students just watch and listen. Be sure to use a natural speaking voice, and good rhythm and intonation.

2. **Say the word and the article that goes with it several times**, as you indicate the object. For example, say: *a bathroom, a bathroom, a bathroom*. Have your students then repeat the word after you several times.

3. **Say the word in the same sentence again.** Have students repeat

after you each time, "This is a bathroom."

4. **Check students' comprehension by asking direct questions**. For example, *What is this? Where's the ball? Is this a bottle?*

Listen and repeat.

Question	
How are	you?
How is	he? she? it?

Answer
Fine.
Fine.

2A. Grammar

Model, Repeat and Solo the pronunciation of all forms shown on the chart.

Note: **Fine** or **Good** are common responses to the question, **How are you?**

Listen and repeat.

I need _____.

Pronoun		
I	need	some water.
You	need	some food.
He/She/It	needs	a bathroom.
You/We/They	need	help.

2B. Grammar

Model, Repeat, and Solo the pronunciation of all forms shown on the chart.

> **Listen and repeat.**
>
> A: Hello, **Jane**! How **are you**?
>
> B: **I need help. I need water**, please.
>
> A: Yes, of course! Here is a **bottle of water**!
>
> B: Thank you.

3A. Conversation 1:

1. **Model: Say both parts of the conversation several times.** Use A and B cards, stick figures, or change your physical position to indicate the dual parts. Role-play the parts to convey the meaning of the conversation. **Students are to watch and listen.**

2. **Repeat: Say one line at a time and have students repeat until they can be understood.**

3. **Solo: You begin the conversation and call on individual students to respond.** Then reverse the roles (students are A, you are B).

4. Once students can do both parts, **encourage free conversation** (students substitute their own words for the blue words).

03-10

> # Listen and repeat.
>
> A: Hi **Bob**. Are you OK? What do you need?
>
> B: I need **some food**.
>
> A: Well, let's go **to eat**.
>
> B: Yes, let's go!
>
> ©2020-2021 Literacy International

3B. Conversation 2

1. **Model: Say both parts of the conversation several times.** Use A and B cards, stick figures, or change your physical position to indicate the dual parts. Role play the parts to convey the meaning of the conversation. **Students are to watch and listen.**

2. **Repeat: Say one line at a time and have students repeat until they can be understood.**

3. **Solo: You begin the conversation and call on individual students to respond.** Then reverse the roles (students are A, you are B).

4. Once students can do both parts, **encourage free conversation** (students substitute their own words for the blue words).

Listen and repeat.

1. /A/	2. /b/	3. Challenge
table	bye	
name	bottle	
OK	bathroom	
play	ball	
8	Bible	

A. OK, I need 8 bottles.
B. The Bible is on the table.

4A. Pronunciation- Sound and Spelling

1. **Model: Say the sound several times while pointing to it.** (For example, point to the **b** and say /b/ /b/ /b/. **Then say the sound and quickly read the entire list, pointing to each item as you read it** (/b/ bye, bottle, bathroom, ball, Bob). Students just watch and listen.

2. **Repeat: Say the sound and each word several times, having students repeat each time after you in unison.** Be sure to use your normal voice and rate of speed. Do one column at a time, top to bottom. Then read the two sentences.

3. **Solo: Call on individuals to say a sound and its word group.** Give lots of praise.

4. **Challenge:** Choose another sound from the lesson that is challenging for your particular students to pronounce. Use words

from Parts 1 and 2 of the lesson, and from previous lessons to make a group of 3-5 words. You may repeat the same challenging sounds in several lessons. Students need a lot of practice on sounds that do not exist in their first language.

Listen and repeat.

—	—	—
	-	-
food	water	I need
bad	bottle	hello
ball	table	goodbye
fork	never	let's go
bread	thirsty	repeat

4B. Hum and clap the stress.

Begin by humming the stress of a column of words. Hum higher, longer and louder for big dashes, lower, shorter and quieter for small dashes.

You may use hand gestures to indicate that **the stressed syllable is higher in pitch, longer in duration and louder.** Invite your students to join in humming the rhythm. Once the class is humming the rhythm in unison, you can begin saying the words. You may also wish to clap the syllables while you say the words.

1. Model: Hum and then say each word in the group several times. Students listen.
2. Repeat: students repeat words after you in unison.
3. Solo: call on individuals to read the entire group of words.

> **God is our Father**
> Matthew 6:9
>
> So this is how you should pray: "Our Father in heaven, we pray that your name will always be kept holy."

5A. Bible Reading

Students have already read this verse in their native language as part of their homework, so it will be familiar even if they do not know all the vocabulary yet. The pictures also help them to understand. The hyperlink of the Bible verse will take you to https://live.bible.is/ where you can select from over 1,000 languages to read and listen to the verse and watch the video, if you wish.

A. Read the verse out loud to the class.

B. Write words that students ask about and give simple definitions.

C. Ask for volunteers to read aloud the verse.

D. Ask if there are any questions or comments about the verse. The picture is Jesus praying to his father, God.

E. You may also ask simple questions if student's ability permits: Who is in the picture? Who is our father?

> But anyone who drinks the water I give will never be thirsty again...
>
> John 4:14 ERV

5B. Bible Reading

Students have already read this verse in their native language as part of their homework, so it will be familiar even if they do not know all the vocabulary yet. The pictures also help them to understand. The hyperlink of the Bible verse will take you to https://live.bible.is/ where you can select from over 1,000 languages to read and listen to the verse and watch the video, if you wish.

A. Read the verse out loud to the class.

B. Write words that students ask about and give simple definitions.

C. Ask for volunteers to read aloud the verse.

D. Ask if there are any questions or comments about the verse.

E. You may also ask simple questions if student's ability permits: Who is in the picture? Who can drink the water Jesus gives?

Listen and write one word per line.

1.
2.
3.
4.
5.
6.
7.

OK
bottle
bad
bathroom
name
table
ball

6A Activities - Dictation of sound/spelling words

Read the words with a sample sentence and have students write just one word for each line. Check spelling.

For more advanced students, you can hide the sample word bank.

1. name, name (What is your name?) name
2. bottle, bottle (Here is a bottle of water.) bottle
3. OK, OK (I'm OK.) OK
4. table, table (The fork is on the table.) table
5. bathroom, bathroom (He is in the bathroom.) bathroom
6. ball, ball (Let's play with a ball.) ball
7. bad, bad (The food is bad.) bad

What do they need?

6B. Activities

Students will answer the question with complete sentences.

Their answers may vary.
1. He needs to drink. Or He needs water.
2. He needs food. Or He needs to eat.
3. He needs a bathroom.
4. She needs help.
5. She needs help.

> # Song - Living Water
>
> I need water.
> And I need food.
> I need his help
> And I know you do, too. (2X)
>
> Jesus is the Living Water.
> Jesus is the Bread of Life.
> Jesus loves us and he helps us.
> He gives us eternal life.

7. Song
Students will learn the new song for the lesson and may also request to sing favorite songs from previous lessons, if time permits.

1. Model: Read the song lyrics out loud to the class. Ask if there are any questions. Write on board words that students ask about and give simple definitions Then sing it two or three times, as the students just listen.

2. Repeat: Sing the selection again, a line or sentence at a time, as students repeat after you. Then play the recording and sing the song together as a class in unison.

3. Solo: The student sings solo (or if shy, can just read the words aloud).

> # 1 & 2 Homework
>
> 1. Read the next lesson's Bible verses: Psalm 116:5 and Psalm 147:1 in your language.
>
> 2. Write 6 new words.
>
> A. Need
> B.
> C.
> D.
> E.
> F.
> G.

Homework 1 and 2 - Reading the next Bible Lesson in L1, and writing about self with new vocabulary

Students will always read the Bible lesson in their first language (L1) before reading it in English the following lesson. Help them get a Bible in their own language if they don't have one. They may also use Bible.is, ScriptureEarth.org, BibleGateway.com, or other Bible translation resources.

Model. Go over each of the homework assignments to be sure the student understands what to do.

Repeat. Encourage students to find someone with whom to practice conversing and reading the completed homework assignment. They may use a bilingual dictionary.

Solo. Students will share their homework when they are finished. After they have shared their homework, be sure to check it for correctness, including spelling. Explain mistakes, while providing praise and encouragement. Answers will vary.

3. Write the words for each picture.

1 water	2	3	4	5	6
7	8	9	10	11	12

Homework 3 – Write the vocabulary words with the pictures

This homework practices writing. Number one is an example.
1. water
2. to help, Please help.
3. food
4. a table, tables
5. to drink, I drink water.
6. to eat, We eat food.
7. a spoon, spoons
8. a fork, forks
9. a bathroom, bathrooms
10. a bottle, bottles
11. a ball, balls
12. bread

4. Write and say the sentences

A. Hello, my name is Bob.	
B. Let's play ball.	
C. Goodbye, Jane.	
D. The food is on the table.	
E. She is in the bathroom.	

Homework 4 – Write and say sentences with the new sounds.

This homework practices writing, spelling and pronouncing the /A/ and /b/ sounds.

03-21

> # 5. Homework
>
> Write the Bible verses.
>
> 1. So this is how you should pray: "Our Father in heaven, we pray that your name will always be kept holy." (Matthew 6:9 ERV)
>
> 2. But anyone who drinks the water I give will never be thirsty again... (John 4:14, ERV)

Homework 5 – Bible Story Review

Copy the Bible verses from the lesson.

> # 6. Homework – Choose 1 Verse to Memorize
>
> **A**
>
> So this is how you should pray: "Our Father in heaven, we pray that your name will always be kept holy." (Matthew 6:9 ERV)
>
> **B**
>
> But anyone who drinks the water I give will never be thirsty again… (John 4:14, ERV)

Homework 6 – Memorize a Verse

Learners get to choose A, B, to memorize. Please notice that the memory work is not long. Everyone, regardless of skill level, should be able to do it.

1. **Model.** Recite a verse from memory.

2. **Repeat.** Encourage students to find someone with whom to practice conversing and reading the completed homework assignment.

3. **Solo.** Students will recite the verse from memory at the next class.

7. Homework

need   **needs**

A. I _____ water.
B. They _____ food.
C. He _____ help.
D. We _____ love.
E. It _____ a name.
F. She _____ a spoon.

©2020-2021 Literacy International

Homework 7 – Grammar Review

1. Use the words provided to fill in the blanks. To model, write "I need water."

Answers:
A. need
B. need
C. needs
D. need
E. needs
F. needs

03-24

> ## 8. Homework - Memorize and practice with a friend.
>
> A: Hey! How are you doing?
> B: I need help. I need water, please.
> A: Yes, of course! Here is a bottle of water!
> B: Thank you.

Homework 8 – Everyday Reading and Writing.

Memorize the conversation and practice with a partner. Students my substitute the words in blue with their own words.

9. Homework- Write your answers

List the things you need now.

1. I need water.
2. I need _____.
3. I need _____.
4. I need _____.
5. I need _____.

Homework 9 – Writing about theme or Bible Story

Model. Example - I need water. Answers will vary.

10. Homework - Now I Can…

- ❏ I can say the things I need.
- ❏ I can understand, say, read, and write the 12 vocabulary words.
- ❏ I can ask "How are you?" and reply "Fine."
- ❏ I understand that God is our father.

Homework 10 – I can statements

The student must be able to achieve all of these skills before the next lesson. If not, the lesson can be repeated or additional practice materials (see notes on slide 1) can be used.

Review all of the skills at the beginning of the next lesson. Be sure to give lots of praise and encouragement!

Closing Prayer

Pray
You may want to ask for any special prayer requests, then pray for your students and bless them.

Light of the World
Learning English through the Bible
Lesson A1-04
©2020-2021 Literacy International

Teacher's Notes:

Bible Reading: God is Good - Psalm 116:5 and 147:1
Theme: Personal Information
Pronunciation: /d/ and /n/
Grammar:
- Am, is
- What's your ___?
- My, your, his, her

Preparation:
- Pray
- Read Psalm 116:5 and 147:1
- Preview slides
- Optional: Bring identification cards, addressed labels or envelopes, forms, birth certificates, etc.

> # Pray, Review, and Preview
>
> **Bible Reading:** God is Good - Psalm 116:5 and 147:1
> **Theme:** Personal Information
> **Pronunciation:** /d/ and /n/
> **Grammar:**
> - Am, is
> - What's your ___?
> - My, your, his, her
>
> ©2020-2021 Literacy International

Pray

Pray for the class. You may want to thank the Lord for your unique students and for his goodness.

Check Homework and Review

Ask each student to read aloud or recite their homework from the last class. Check written work. Be sure they have read Psalm 116:5 and 147:1 in their native languages in preparation for the lesson. The hyperlinks of the Bible verses will take you to https://live.bible.is/ where you can select from over 1,000 languages to read and listen to the verses.

Review the main points of the previous lesson and ask if there are any questions.

What do you see?

DRIVER LICENSE
DOB 01/01/1984
EXPIRES 01/01/2020 CLASS C
FN Ben MN James SEX M
LN Green HGT 5'-8"
489 Good St. HAIR BRN
Chicago, IL WGT 184 lb
60987 EYES BLU
DL F28938203

Registration Form
First Name: Noah
Middle Name: Dan
Last Name: Lee
Email: Lee@Dmail.com
Phone Number: 217-555-1234
Birth Date: 06/09/1999
Address: 123 New St. Newton, NY 23574
Languages: French, English, Ga
Photo:

©2020-2021 Literacy International

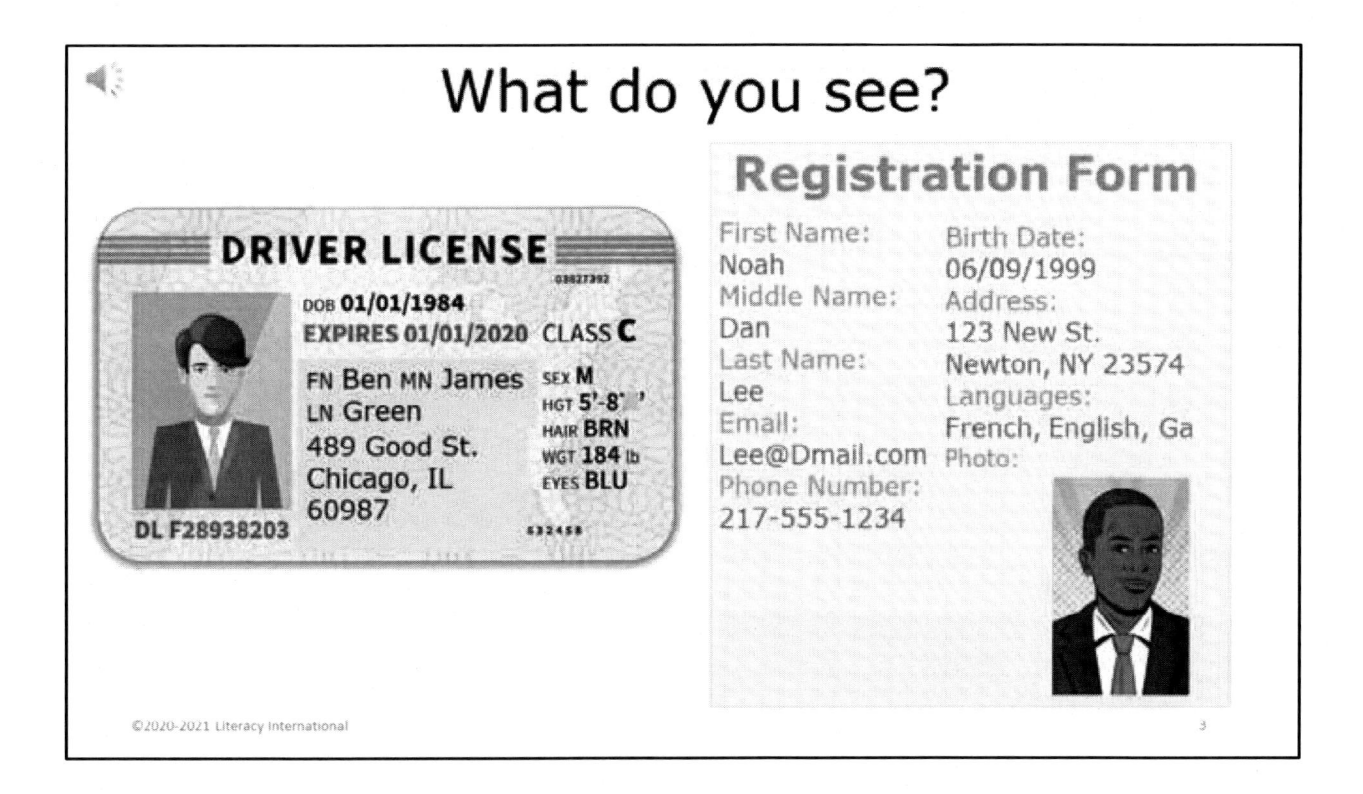

1A. Discuss Theme Picture

- Ask "What do you see in this picture?" and "What else?" to elicit vocabulary they already know.
- Repeat and write their words

Answers may include: name, email, address, ID card, etc.

More advanced students can be encouraged to make complete sentences:
This is a registration form for Noah Lee.

Listen and repeat.

1	2	3	4
Mr. ⟨Noah⟩ Dan Lee	Mr. Noah ⟨Dan⟩ Lee	Mr. Noah Dan ⟨Lee⟩	123 New St. Newton, NY USA
a first name	a middle name	a last name	an address
first names	middle names	last names	addresses

©2020-2021 Literacy International

2A. Vocabulary

1. **Say the new words in a simple sentence: "This is a first name."** several times, while indicating the object or picture. Students just watch and listen. Be sure to use a natural speaking voice, and good rhythm and intonation.

2. **Say the word and the article that goes with it several times**, as you indicate the object. For example, say: *a first name, a first name.* Have your students then repeat the word after you several times.

3. **Say the word in the same sentence again**. Have students repeat after you each time, "This is a first name."

4. **Check students' comprehension by asking direct questions**. For example, *What is this? Where's the last name? Is this an address?*

Listen and repeat.

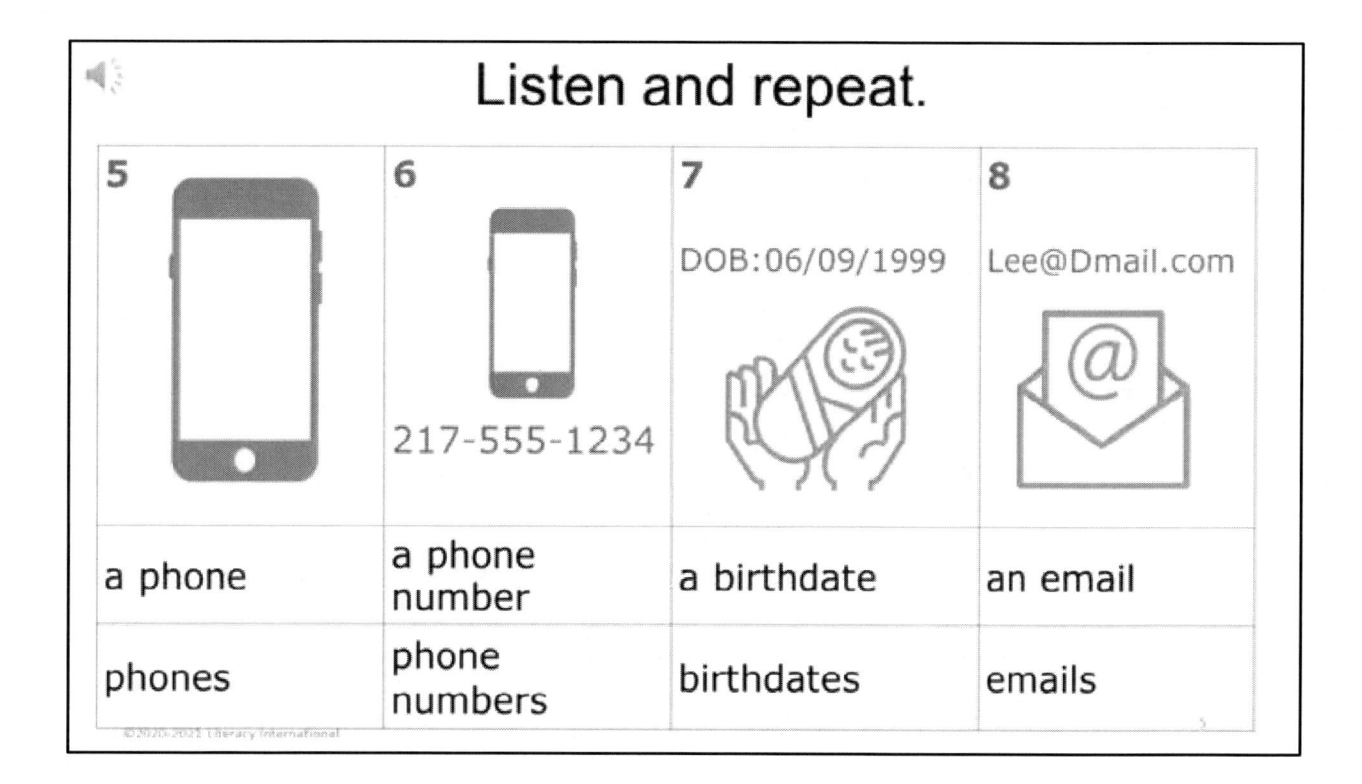

5	6	7	8
[phone image]	[phone image] 217-555-1234	DOB:06/09/1999 [baby image]	Lee@Dmail.com [email image]
a phone	a phone number	a birthdate	an email
phones	phone numbers	birthdates	emails

2B. Vocabulary

Note: The symbols in an email address are pronounced "at" for @ and "dot" for the period.
DOB stands for Date of Birth.

1. **Say the new words in a simple sentence: "This is a phone."** several times, while indicating the object or picture. Students just watch and listen. Be sure to use a natural speaking voice, and good rhythm and intonation.

2. **Say the word and the article that goes with it several times**, as you indicate the object. For example, say: *a phone, a phone.* Have your students then repeat the word after you several times.

3. **Say the word in the same sentence again**. Have students repeat after you each time, "This is a phone."

4. **Check students' comprehension by asking direct questions**. For example, *What is this? Where's the phone number? Is this an email?*

04-5

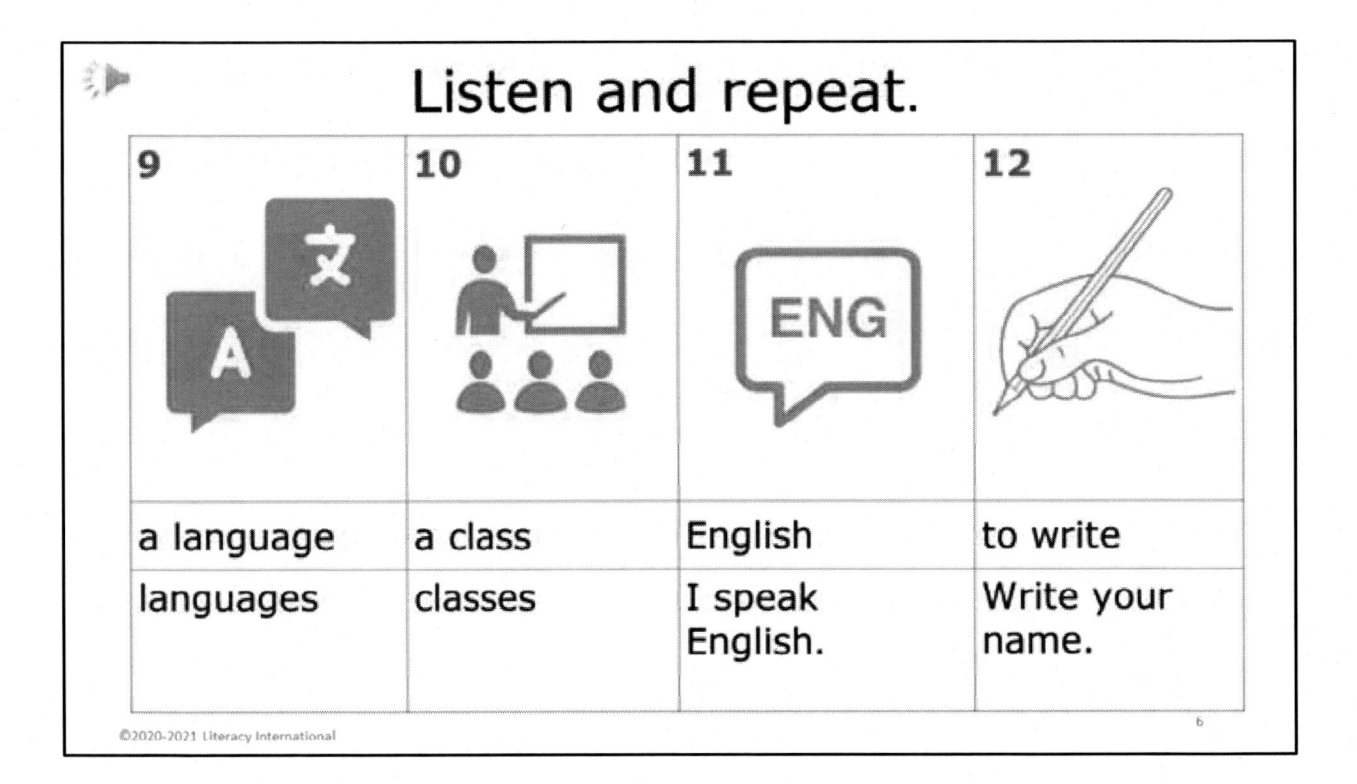

9	10	11	12
a language	a class	English	to write
languages	classes	I speak English.	Write your name.

2C. Vocabulary

1. **Say the new words in a simple sentence: "This is a language."** several times, while indicating the object or picture. Students just watch and listen. Be sure to use a natural speaking voice, and good rhythm and intonation.

2. **Say the word and the article that goes with it several times**, as you indicate the object. For example, say: *a language, a language.* Have your students then repeat the word after you several times.

3. **Say the word in the same sentence again**. Have students repeat after you each time, "This is a language."

4. **Check students' comprehension by asking direct questions**. For example, *What is this? Where's a class? Is this a language?*

Listen and repeat.

Question ?		Answer
What is your What's your	name?	Sara Smith
	address?	321 Green Street, London
	phone number?	708-487-9870
	birthdate?	May 1, 1999
	email?	Sara@Dmail.com
	first language?	French

2D. Grammar

Spoken English usually uses the contraction forms. Written English usually uses the full forms.

Model, Repeat, and Solo the pronunciation of all forms shown on the chart.

Listen and repeat.

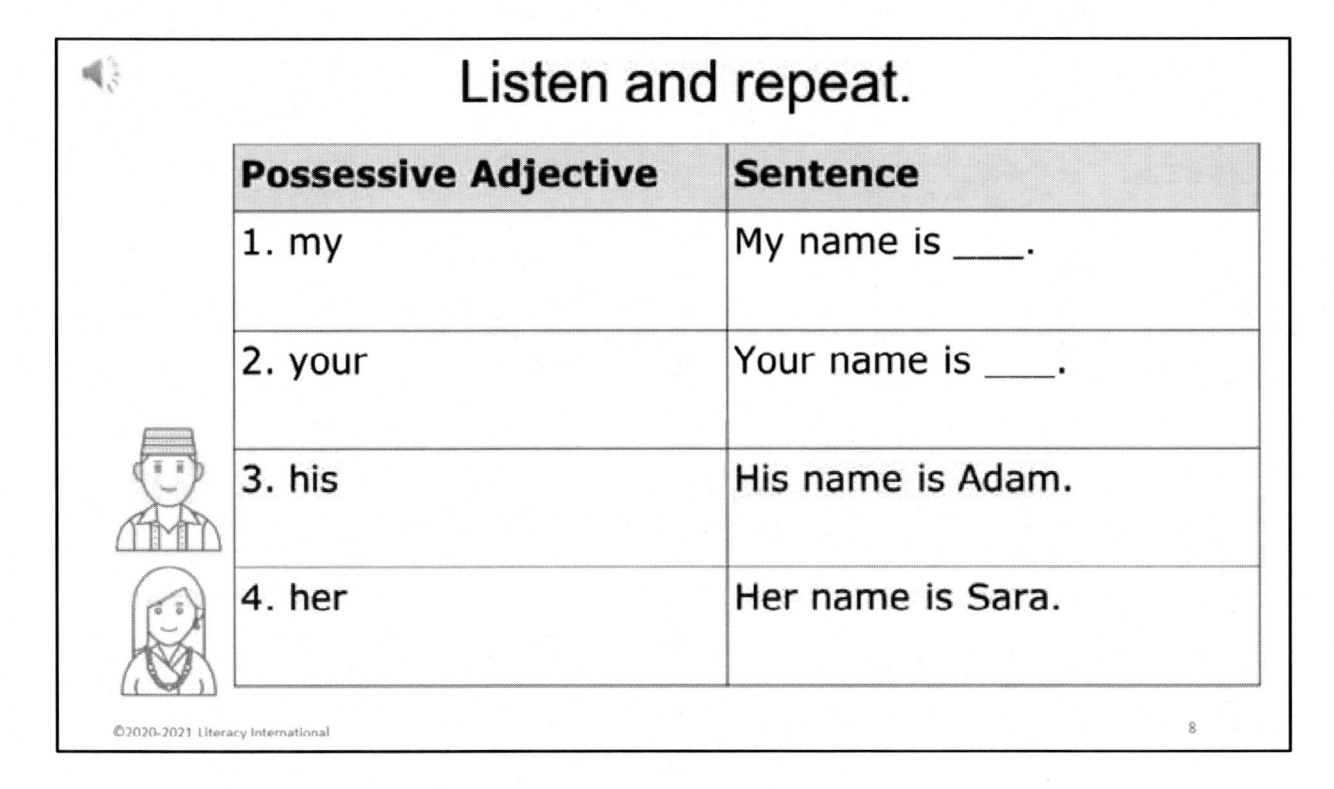

Possessive Adjective	Sentence
1. my	My name is ___.
2. your	Your name is ___.
3. his	His name is Adam.
4. her	Her name is Sara.

2E. Grammar

Model, Repeat, and Solo the pronunciation of all forms shown on the chart.

Model: Gesture to yourself for "My name is___" and gesture to your student for "Your name is___."
Point to the man for "his" and to the woman for "her".

Repeat: Have the student repeat the sentences but be sure they use their own name for 1 and your name for 2.

Solo: The student reads all sentences alone.

> # Listen and repeat.
>
> A: Welcome to English class! What's your name?
>
> B: My name is Joe.
>
> A: Hi Joe! What's your phone number?
>
> B: My phone number is 312-555-2098.
>
> A: What's your birthdate?
>
> B: My birthdate is 9-12-99.

3A. Conversation

1. **Model: Say both parts of the conversation several times.** Use A and B cards, stick figures, or change your physical position to indicate the dual parts. Role-play the parts to convey the meaning of the conversation. **Students are to watch and listen.**

2. **Repeat: Say one line at a time and have students repeat until they can be understood.**

3. **Solo: You begin the conversation and call on individual students to respond.** Then reverse the roles (students are A, you are B).

4. Once students can do both parts, **encourage free conversation** (students substitute their own words for the blue words and answer truthfully).

Listen and repeat.

1. /d/	2. /n/	3. Challenge
day	name	
date	number	
do	no	
birthdate	nice	
address	phone	

1. Your name is nice.
2. No, I do not need the address.

4A. Pronunciation- Sound and Spelling

1. **Model: Say the sound several times while pointing to it.** (For example, point to the **d** and say /d/ /d/ /d/. **Then say the sound and quickly read the entire list, pointing to each item as you read it** (/d/ day, date, do, birthdate, address). Students just watch and listen.

2. **Repeat: Say the sound and each word several times, having students repeat each time after you in unison.** Be sure to use your normal voice and rate of speed. Do one column at a time, top to bottom. Then read the sentences at the bottom.

3. **Solo: Call on individuals to say a sound and its word group.** Give lots of praise.

4. **Challenge:** Choose another sound from the lesson that is challenging for your particular students to pronounce. Use words

04-10a

from Parts 1 and 2 of the lesson, and from previous lessons to make a group of 3-5 words. You may repeat the same challenging sounds in several lessons. Students need a lot of practice on sounds that do not exist in their first language.

Listen and repeat.

—	— -	— - -
name	address	phone number
phone	number	addresses
last	email	languages
first	birthdate	middle name

4B. Hum and clap the stress.

Begin by humming the stress of a column of words. Hum higher, longer and louder for big dashes, lower, shorter and quieter for small dashes.

You may use hand gestures to indicate that **the stressed syllable is higher in pitch, longer in duration and louder.** Invite your students to join in humming the rhythm. Once the class is humming the rhythm in unison, you can begin saying the words. You may also wish to clap the syllables while you say the words.

1. Model: Hum and then say each word in the group several times. Students listen.
2. Repeat: Students repeat words after you in unison.
3. Solo: Call on individuals to read the entire group of words.

> **God is Good**
> Psalm 116:5 and 147:1
>
> The LORD is good and merciful; our God is so kind.
> Psalm 116:5 ERV
>
> Praise the LORD because he is good. Sing praises to our God. It is good and pleasant to praise him.
> Psalm 147:1 ERV
>
> ©2020-2021 Literacy International   12

5. Bible Reading

Students have already read these scriptures in their native language as part of their homework, so it will be familiar even if they do not know all the vocabulary yet. The picture also helps them to understand. The hyperlink of the Bible verse will take you to https://live.bible.is/ where you can select from over 1,000 languages to read and listen to the verse.

A. Read the verses out loud to the class.

B. Write on board words that students ask about and give simple definitions.

C. Ask for volunteers to read aloud the verses.

D. Ask questions if students' levels are high enough to understand:
Who is good?
Who is kind?
How can we praise him?
Ask if there are any questions or comments about the verses.

Listen and write one word per line.

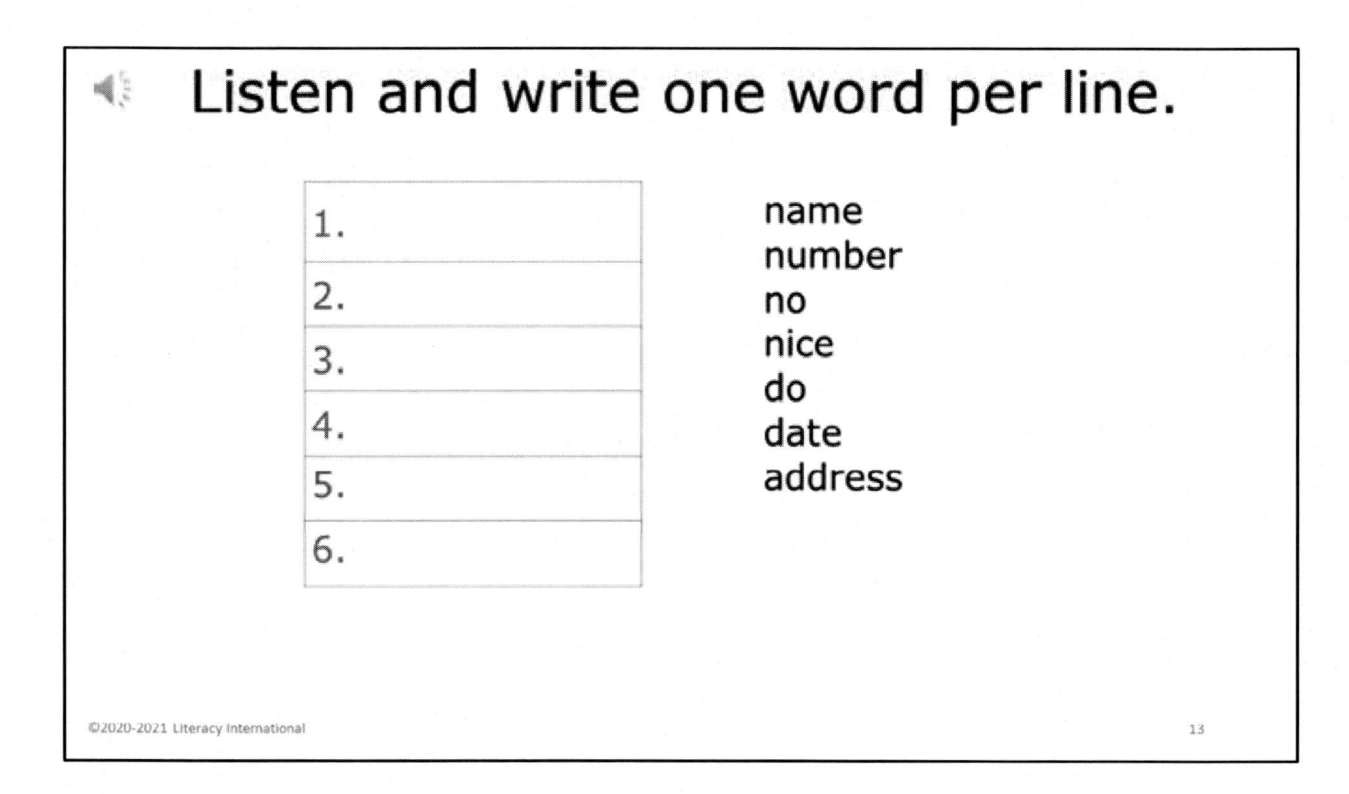

1.
2.
3.
4.
5.
6.

name
number
no
nice
do
date
address

6A. Activities - Dictation of sound/spelling words

Read the words with a sample sentence and have students write just one word for each line. Check spelling.

For more advanced students, you can hide the sample word bank.

1. Name, name, What is your name? Name.
2. Address, address, What's your address? Address.
3. Do, do, Do you need help? Do.
4. Number, number, What's your number? Number
5. Nice, nice, Nice to meet you. Nice.
6. No, no, No, I don't need help. No.

Say and write your partner's answers.

Questions	My partner's answers
1. What's your first name?	
2. What's your middle name?	
3. What's your last name?	
4. What's your email address?	
5. What's your phone number?	
6. What's your birthdate?	
7. What's your address?	

6B. Activities - Pair work

1. Model question 1 as an example.

2. Have each student ask, and write answer their partners' answers. Then switch and the other partner will ask the questions.

3. Check answers.

[Slide image with four people labeled A, B, C, D:
- A: Woman saying "I'm Eve!"
- B: Man with "Adam@Dmail.com"
- C: Woman with "543-321-2300"
- D: Man with "123 Main Street, Sydney"

Questions:
1. What's his address?
2. What's her name?
3. What's his email?
4. What's her phone number?
5. What's your birthdate?
6. What's my name?]

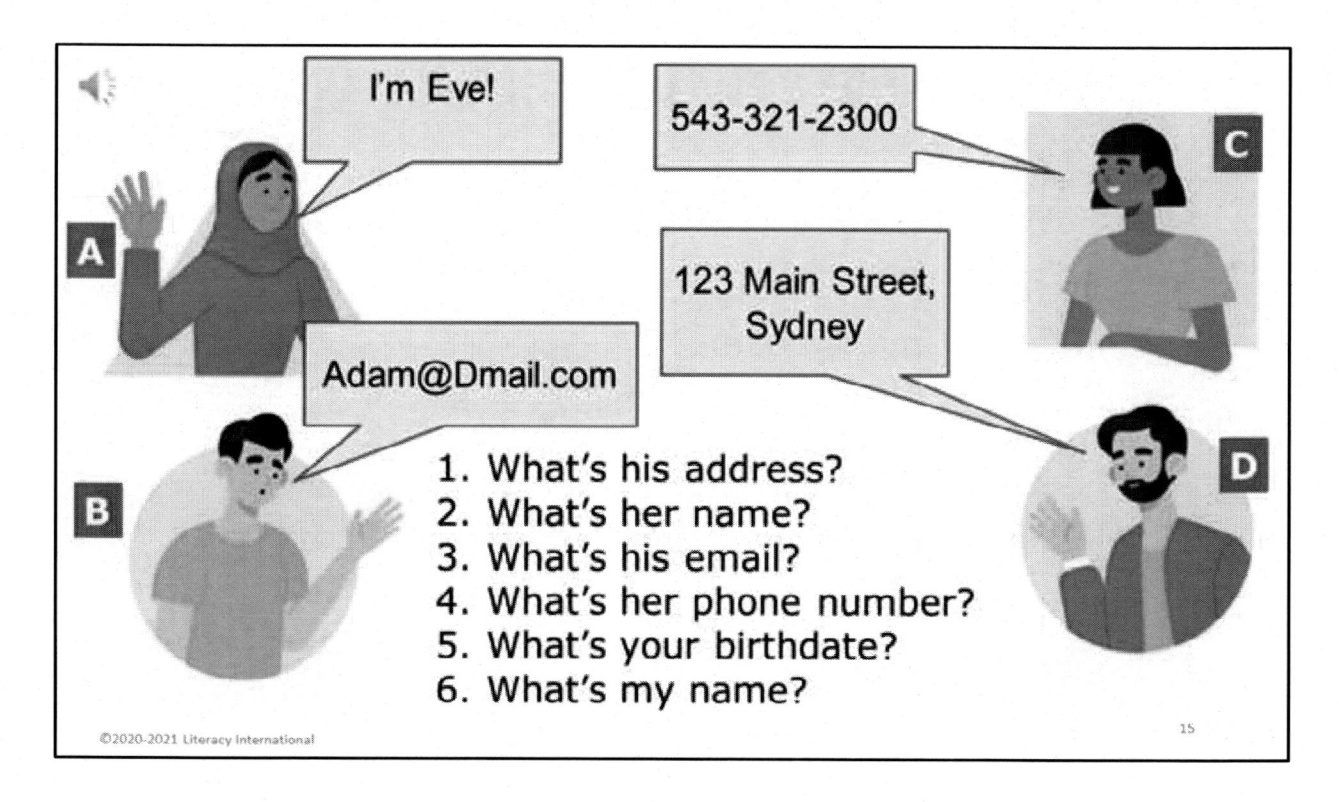

6C. Activities – Pair work – My, Your, His, Her

1. Model: Ask students, "What's **his** address? What's **his** address?" Point to picture D to elicit the student response, "**His** address is 123 Main Street, Sydney."

2. Repeat: Students ask question 1 and give answer D again.

3. Solo: One partner will ask the questions, and the other will give the answers according to the slide pictures. Then switch and the other person asks the questions.

04-15

> # Song - God is so Good!
>
> God is so good.
> God is so good.
> God is so good.
> He's so good to me!
>
> God is so good.
> God is so good.
> God is so good.
> He's so good to me!

7. Song

Students will learn the song and may also sing other songs, if time permits.

1. Model: Read the song lyrics out loud to the class. Ask if there are any questions. Give simple definitions for any words that students ask about. Then sing it two or three times, as the students just listen.

2. Repeat: Sing the selection again, a line or sentence at a time, as students repeat after you. Then play the recording and sing the song together as a class in unison.

3. Solo: The student sings solo (or if shy, can just read the words aloud).

> # 1 & 2 Homework
>
> 1. Read the next lesson's Bible verses: <u>Genesis 1:1-31</u> in your language.
>
> 2. Write 6 sentences. Use name, birthdate, phone number, email, language, my, your, last, first, **and more.**
>
> A. My first language is Mandarin.
> B.
> C.
> D.
> E.
> F.
> G.

8. Homework 1, and 2 - Reading the next Bible Lesson in L1, and writing about self with new vocabulary

Students will always read the Bible lesson in their first language (L1) before reading it in English the following lesson. Help them get a Bible in their own language if they don't have one. The hyperlink of the Bible verse will take you to https://live.bible.is/ where you can select from over 1,000 languages to read and listen to the verses.

Model. Go over each of the **8 homework assignments** to be sure the student understands what to do.

Repeat. Encourage students to find someone with whom to practice conversing and reading the completed homework assignment. They may use a bilingual dictionary.

Solo. Students will share their homework when they are finished. After they have shared their homework, be sure to check it for correctness, including spelling. Explain mistakes, while providing praise and encouragement. Answers will vary.

3. Write the words for each picture.

1 Mr. (Noah) Dan Lee	2 Mr. Noah Dan (Lee)	3 Mr. Noah (Dan) Lee	4 123 New St. Newton, NY	5	6 ENG
a first name					
first names					
7 DOB:06/09/99	8	9	10 312-555-1212	11 Lee@Dmail.com	12

Homework 3 – Write the vocabulary words with the pictures

This homework practices writing the vocabulary words.
Number one is an example.

1. a first name, first names
2. a last name, last names
3. a middle name, middle names
4. an address, addresses
5. a class, classes
6. English
7. a birthdate, birthdates
8. a language, languages
9. a phone, phones
10. a phone number, phone numbers
11. an email address, email addresses
12. to write, Write your name.

04-18

4. Write and say the sentences

A. Your name is nice.	
B. No, I do not need the address.	
C. Adam and Dan need food.	
D. My new number is 979-999-7979.	
E. The bread is bad.	
F. God is good.	

Homework 4 – Write and say sentences with the new sounds.

This homework practices writing, spelling, and pronouncing the /d/ and /n/ sounds.

> ### 🔊 5. Homework – Fill in the blanks.
>
> **God** **good** **good** **good** **God**
>
> 1. The LORD is ___ and merciful; our ___ is so kind.
> Psalm 116:5 ERV
>
> 2. Praise the LORD because he is ___. Sing praises to our ___. It is ___ and pleasant to praise him.
> Psalm 147:1 ERV

Homework 5 – Bible Reading Review

Students may look back at the Bible verses to answer the questions

Answers:
1. The LORD is **good** and merciful; our **God** is so kind.
2. Praise the LORD because he is **good**. Sing praises to our **God**. It is **good** and pleasant to praise him.

04-20

> ### 6. Homework – Choose 1 Verse to Memorize
>
> **A**
> The LORD is good and merciful; our God is so kind.
> Psalm 116:5 ERV
>
> **B**
> Praise the LORD because he is good. Sing praises to our God. It is good and pleasant to praise him.
> Psalm 147:1 ERV

Homework 6 – Memorize a Verse

Learners get to choose A, B, or C (on the next slide) to memorize. Please notice that the memory work is not long. Everyone, regardless of skill level, should be able to do it.

1. **Model.** Recite a verse from memory.

2. **Repeat.** Encourage students to find someone with whom to practice conversing and reading the completed homework assignment.

3. **Solo.** Students will recite the verse from memory at the next class.

> **6. Homework – Choose 1 Verse to Memorize**
>
> **C**
>
> Give thanks to the LORD because he is good.
> His faithful love will last forever.
> 1 Chronicles 16:34 ERV

Homework 6 – Memorize a Verse

Learners get to choose A, B, (from previous slide) or C to memorize.

7. Homework – Fill in the blanks

name **phone** **last**
email **address** **number**

A. His first _____ is John.

B. My _____ is Adam@Dmail.com.

C. Her phone _____ is 312-588-2300.

D. My _____ is 123 Main Street, Accra.

E. What's your _____ number?

F. What's her _____ name?

Homework 7 – Grammar Review

Use the words provided to fill in the blanks.
Answers:
A. name
B. email
C. number
D. address
E. phone
F. last

8. Homework- Answer questions about Mr. Green on the next slide.

DRIVER LICENSE
03827392
DOB 01/01/1984
EXPIRES 01/01/2020 CLASS **C**
SEX **M**
Ben James Green HGT **5'-8"**
489 Good Street HAIR **BRN**
Chicago, IL WGT **184 lb**
60987 EYES **BLU**
DL **F28938203** CF 18235098796901235789632458

©2020-2021 Literacy International

Homework 8A. – Everyday Reading and Writing.

The learners will read the driver license and answer the questions on the next slide.

8. Homework- Answer questions about Mr. Green.

1. What's his first name?	
2. What's his birthdate?	
3. What's his address?	
4. What's his last name?	
5. What's his middle name?	

Homework 8B. – Everyday Reading and Writing.

Students will read the driver license on the previous slide and answer the questions.

Answers:
1. Ben
2. 01-01-1984
3. 489 Good Street, Chicago, IL 60987
4. Green
5. James

9. Homework - Write and say your answers

What's your...?

1. first name?	
2. middle name?	
3. last name?	
4. phone number?	
5. birthdate?	
6. email address?	

Homework 9 – Writing about theme

Answers will vary.

> # 10. Homework - Now I Can...
>
> ❑ I can ask and answer personal information questions.
> ❑ I understand my, your, his and her.
> ❑ I can read, write, say, and understand the 12 vocabulary words.
> ❑ I understand that God is good.

Homework 10 – I Can Statements Checklist.

The student must be able to achieve all of these skills before the next lesson. If not, the lesson can be repeated.
Review all of the skills at the beginning of the next lesson. Be sure to give lots of praise and encouragement!

Closing Prayer

Pray

You may want to ask for any special prayer requests, then pray for your students and bless them.

Light of the WORLD
Learning English through the Bible
Lesson A1-05
©2020-2021 Literacy International

Teacher's Notes:

Bible Reading: God is our Creator. Genesis 1:1-31
Theme: People, man, woman, child
Pronunciation: /oo/ and /ch/
Grammar:
- Am/is/are
- Subject pronouns

Preparation:
- Pray
- Read Genesis 1:1-31
- Preview slides and song
- Optional: a chair, toy animals, and dolls

> # Pray, Review, and Preview
>
> **Bible Reading:** God is our Creator. Genesis 1:1-31
> **Theme:** People, man, woman, child
> **Pronunciation:** /oo/ and /ch/
> **Grammar:**
> - Am/is/are
> - Subject pronouns

Pray
Pray for the class. You may want to thank the Lord for people, animals, and his creation.

Check Homework and Review

Ask each student to read aloud or recite their homework from the last class. Check written work. Be sure they have read Genesis 1:1-31 in their native languages in preparation for the lesson.

Review the main points of the previous lesson and ask if there are any questions.

What do you see?

1A. Discuss Theme Picture

- Ask "What do you see in this picture?" and "What else?" to elicit vocabulary they already know.
- Repeat and write their words or show the words on the next slide.

Answers may include: **people, man, woman, girl, boy, children, animal**, which are vocabulary words. Students may already know **husband, wife, parents, kids, dog**. Family vocabulary is introduced in Lesson 23.

More advanced students can be encouraged to make complete sentences:
This is a man. This is a woman. These are children. There are two boys and three girls.

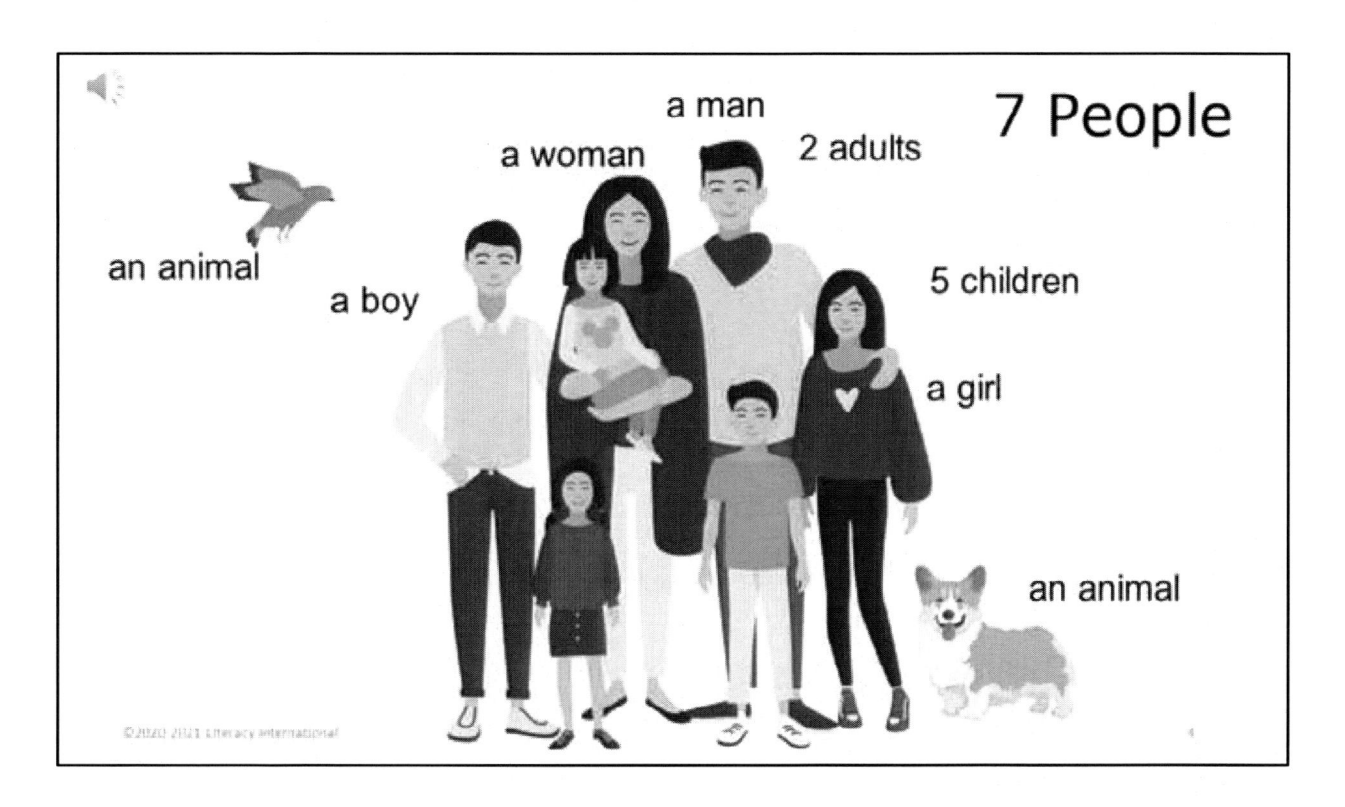

1B. Show Theme Picture Words

Briefly say the words shown. Vocabulary lesson begins on the next slide.

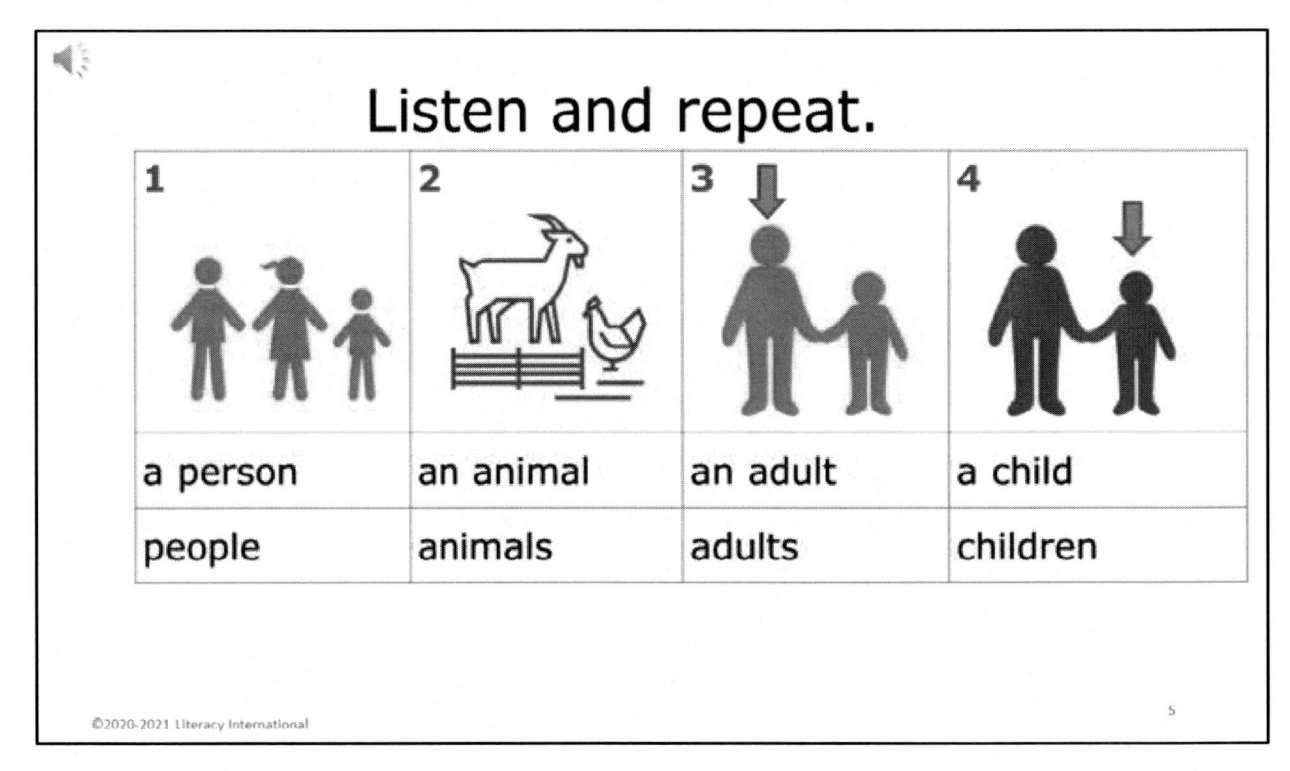

> **Listen and repeat.**
>
> | 1 | 2 | 3 | 4 |
> |---|---|---|---|
> | a person | an animal | an adult | a child |
> | people | animals | adults | children |

2A. Vocabulary

Note on Plurals: Usually plural nouns end in "s" or "es," but **person** changes to **people.** The plurals **men**, **women**, and **children** have irregular spelling and all end in "en" without an "s."

1. **Say the new words in a simple sentence:** "This is a person" several times, while indicating the object or picture. Students just watch and listen. Be sure to use a natural speaking voice, and good rhythm and intonation.

2. **Say the word and the article that goes with it several times**, as you indicate the object. For example, say: *a person, a person, a person*. Have your students then repeat the word after you several times.

3. **Say the word in the same sentence again**. Have students repeat after you each time, "This is a person."

4. **Check students' comprehension by asking direct questions.** For example, What is this? Where's the animal? Is this a child?

Listen and repeat.

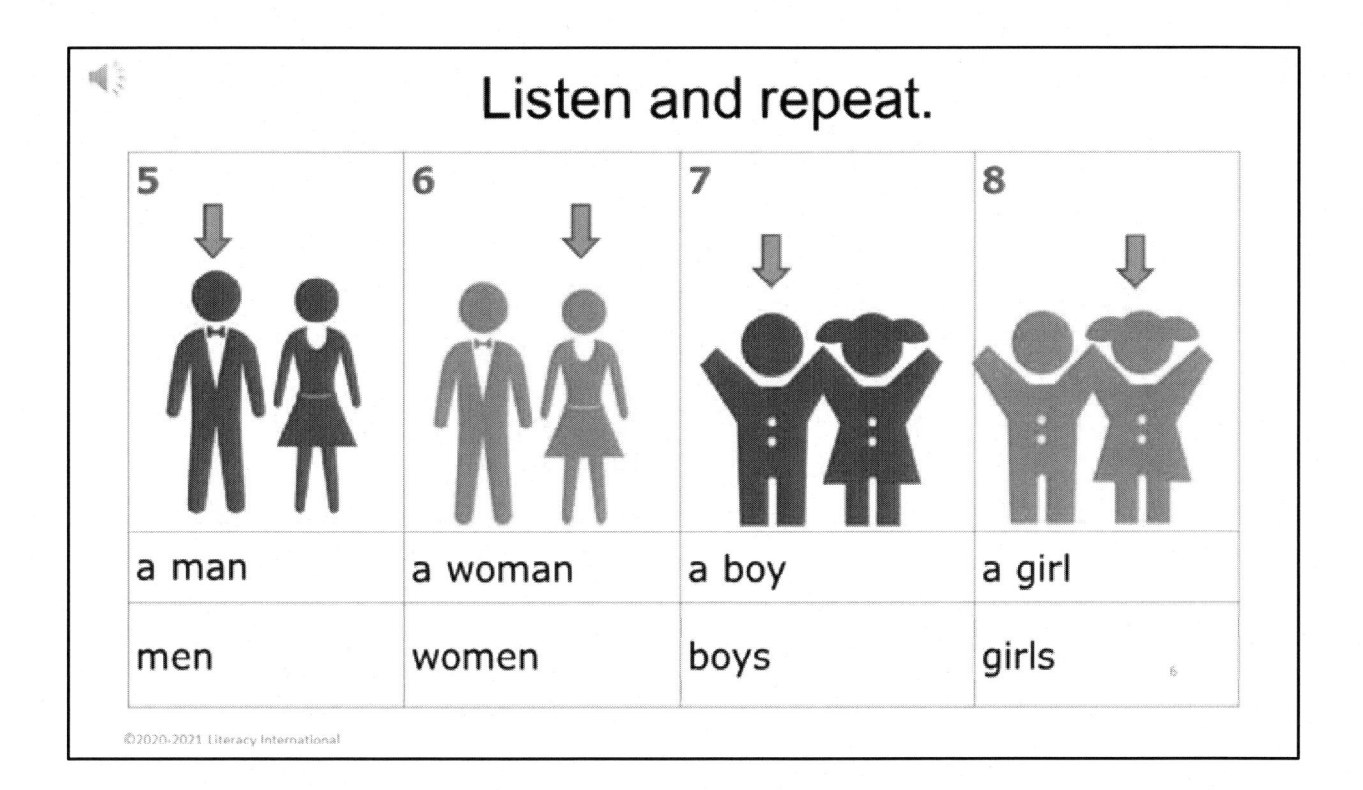

5 — a man	6 — a woman	7 — a boy	8 — a girl
men	women	boys	girls

2B. Vocabulary

Irregular Plurals: Usually plural nouns end in "s" or "es," but **men**, **women**, and **children** have irregular spelling and all end in "en" without an "s."

Note the pronunciation of **woman** (woo-mun) and **women** (wi-mun). Although the letter changes in the second syllable, the pronunciation changes in the first syllable.

Listen and repeat.

9	10	11	12
a friend	an enemy	a chair	to look
friends	enemies	chairs	He looks at the phone.

2C. Vocabulary

1. **Say the new words in a simple sentence:** "They are friends." several times, while indicating the object or picture. Students just watch and listen. Be sure to use a natural speaking voice, and good rhythm and intonation.

2. **Say the word and the article that goes with it several times**, as you indicate the object. For example, say: *a friend, a friend, a friend*. Have your students then repeat the word after you several times.

3. **Say the word in the same sentence again**. Have students repeat after you each time, "They are friends."

4. **Check students' comprehension by asking direct questions**. For example, *What is this? Where's the chair? Is this an enemy?*

> **Look, listen, and repeat.**
>
> I am Joe. I am a man.
>
> You are Liz. You are a woman.

2D. Grammar: Subject Pronouns

Note: "You" can be singular or plural, but is always used with the plural verb form.

1. Model: Say each sentence several times. Students are to watch and listen. Also point to yourself and say your own name, e.g. "I am Mary. I am a woman."

2. Repeat: Say one line at a time and have students repeat until they can be understood.

3. Solo: Call on individual students to say the sentences.

> Look, listen, and repeat.
>
> She is Sue. She is a girl.
>
> He is Jake. He is a boy.

2D. Grammar: Subject Pronouns

1. Model: Say each sentence several times. Students are to watch and listen.

2. Repeat: Say one line at a time and have students repeat until they can be understood.

3. Solo: Call on individual students to say the sentences.

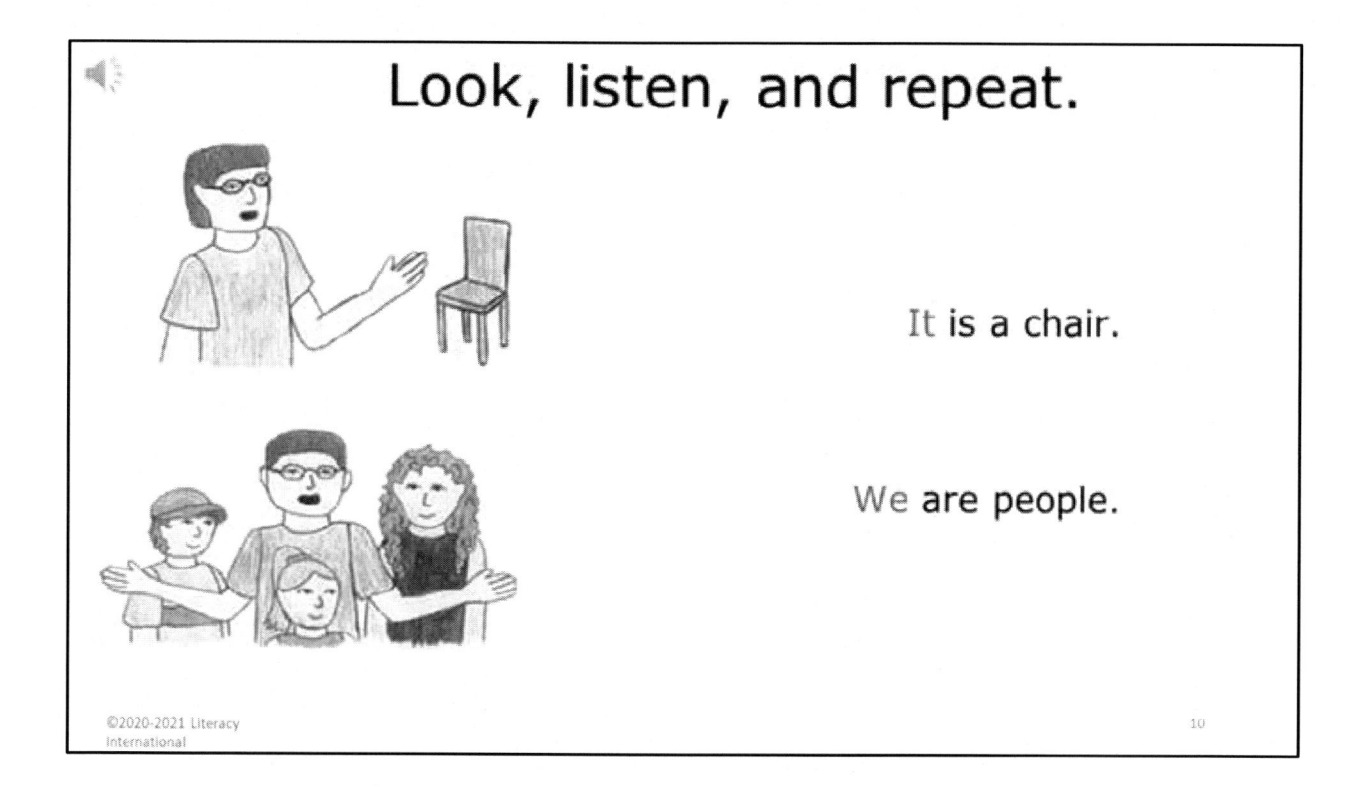

> **Look, listen, and repeat.**
>
> It is a chair.
>
> We are people.

2D. Grammar: Subject Pronouns

Note: The pronoun "it" is used for objects and animals, not for people.

1. Model: Say each sentence several times. Students are to watch and listen.

2. Repeat: Say one line at a time and have students repeat until they can be understood.

3. Solo: Call on individual students to say the sentences.

> **Look, listen, and repeat.**
>
> You are Liz, Sue and Jake. You are people.
>
> They are Sue and Jake. They are children.

2D. Grammar: Subject Pronouns

Note: "You" can be singular or plural, but is always used with the plural verb form.

1. Model: Say each sentence several times. Students are to watch and listen.

2. Repeat: Say one line at a time and have students repeat until they can be understood.

3. Solo: Call on individual students to say the sentences.

Listen and repeat.

	Pronoun	To Be	Sentence
Singular 1	I	am	I am a person.
	you	are	You are a person.
	he she it	is	He is a man. She is a woman. It is an animal.
Plural 2+	we you they	are	We are people. You are people. They are people.

2E. Grammar - Subject Pronouns and Am, Is, Are

Note:
- **Pronouns** are used instead of a noun when the subject is already known.
- **They** can refer to people or objects.

Model, Repeat and Solo the pronunciation of all forms shown on the chart. Discuss the sentences given as examples.

Describe the picture with pronouns.

2F. Grammar and Vocabulary Practice

1. Describe the picture with simple sentences: **He is a man. She is a woman. They are children. They are adults. It is an animal.**
2. Ask the students to describe the picture to you.
3. Ask the students questions:

   Is she a woman?
   Is it a child?
   Are they enemies?

Other words students may ask about are parents, grandparents, ages, family, baby, dog.

> ## Listen and repeat.
>
> A: Hi Joe. Look at my photo.
>
> B. Nice! Who are they?
>
> A. This is Liz. She is my friend.
>
> B: Who is the boy?
>
> A: He is Adam.
>
> B: It is a good photo. Thank you!

3A. Conversation

1. **Model: Say both parts of the conversation several times.** Use A and B cards, stick figures, or change your physical position to indicate the dual parts. Role play the parts to convey the meaning of the conversation. **Students are to watch and listen.**

2. **Repeat: Say one line at a time and have students repeat until they can be understood.**

3. **Solo: You begin the conversation and call on individual students to respond.** Then reverse the roles (students are A, you are B).

4. Once students can do both parts, **encourage free conversation** (students substitute the blue words and answer truthfully). You may encourage students to show their own photos.

05-14

Listen and repeat.

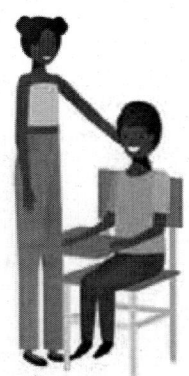

1. /oo/	2. /ch/	3. Challenge
look	chair	
good	church	
book	child	
woman	children	

1. The child is in the chair.
2. The woman looks at a good book.

4A. Pronunciation - Sound and Spelling

1. **Model: Say the sound several times while pointing to it.** (For example, point to the **"oo"** and say /oo/ /oo/ /oo/. **Then say the sound and quickly read the entire list, pointing to each item as you read it** /oo/ look, good, book, woman). Students just watch and listen.

2. **Repeat: Say the sound and each word several times, having students repeat each time after you in unison.** Be sure to use your normal voice and rate of speed. Do one column at a time, top to bottom. Then read the sentences.

3. **Solo: Call on individuals to say a sound and its word group.** Give lots of praise.

4. **Challenge:** Choose another sound from the lesson that is challenging for your particular students to pronounce. Use words

from Parts 1 and 2 of the lesson, and from previous lessons to make a group of 3-5 words. You may repeat the same challenging sounds in several lessons. Students need a lot of practice on sounds that do not exist in their first language.

Listen and repeat.

A. —	B. — -	C. — --
look	children	enemy
boy	woman	animal
girl	person	addresses
child	bathroom	languages

4B. Hum and clap the stress.

Begin by humming the stress of a column of words. Hum higher, longer, and louder for big dashes and lower, shorter, and quieter for small dashes.

You may use hand gestures to indicate that **the stressed syllable is higher in pitch, longer in duration and louder.** Invite your students to join in humming the rhythm. Once the class is humming the rhythm in unison, you can begin saying the words. You may also wish to clap the syllables while you say the words.

1. Model: Hum and then say each word in the group several times. Students listen.
2. Repeat: students repeat words after you in unison.
3. Solo: call on individuals to read the entire column of words.

> **God is our Creator.**
>
> Genesis 1:1
>
> God created the sky and the earth.

5A. Bible Reading:

Students have already read these verses in their native language as part of their homework, so it will be familiar even if they do not know all the vocabulary yet. The pictures also help them to understand. The hyperlink of the Bible verses will take you to https://live.bible.is/ where you can select from over 1,000 languages to read and listen to the verses.

A. Read the story out loud to the class from this slide and the next slide.

B. Write words that students ask about and give simple definitions or translations.

C. Ask for volunteers to read aloud sentences.

D. Ask if there are any questions or comments about the story.

E. Ask simple questions: Who created the sky? Who created the earth? Who is our creator? What did God create?

God is our Creator.
Genesis 1:20-28

God created animals. Last, he created people, as man and woman, to be like Him. He told them to have many children.

©2020-2021 Literacy International

5B. Bible Reading:

Students have already read these verses in their native language as part of their homework, so it will be familiar even if they do not know all the vocabulary yet. The pictures also help them to understand. The hyperlink of the Bible verses will take you to https://live.bible.is/ where you can select from over 1,000 languages to read and listen to the verses.

A. Read the story out loud to the class from this slide and the next slide.

B. Write words that students ask about and give simple definitions or translations.

C. Ask for volunteers to read aloud sentences.

D. Ask if there are any questions or comments about the story.

E. Ask simple questions: Who created animals? Who created people? Who was created like God? What did God create last? What did he tell them to do?

> Listen and write one word per line.

1.
2.
3.
4.
5.
6.
7.

child
book
good
look
woman
children
church

6A. Activities - Dictation of sound/spelling words

Read the words with a sample sentence and have students write just one word for each line. Check spelling.

For more advanced students, you can hide the sample word bank.

1. Child, child (The child is a girl.) child
2. Woman, woman (The woman sits in a chair.) woman
3. Book, book (The Bible is the good book.) book
4. Good, good. (You are a good student.) Good
5. Children, children (The children say goodbye.) children
6. Church, church (The boy goes to church.) church
7. Look, look (Look at the animal.) look

Say the Opposite

A. Words	Opposites	B. Words	Opposites
1. good	bad	8. children	adults
2. hello		9. women	
3. a man		10. animals	
4. an adult		11. an enemy	
5. a boy		12. goodbye	
6. a friend		13. bad	
7. a girl		14. boys	

©2020-2021 Literacy International

6B. Activities - Pair work

First explain opposites by giving examples. "Good (thumbs up), bad (thumbs down), are opposites. Hello (wave and move toward student) Goodbye (wave and move away) are opposites."

Partner A will read words 1-7 and Partner B will say the opposite. Then Partner B will read words 8-14 and Partner A will say the opposite. They may also write the opposites, depending on their skill level.

Answers

1. bad
2. goodbye
3. a woman
4. a child
5. a girl
6. an enemy
7. a boy
8. adults
9. men
10. people
11. a friend
12. hello
13. good
14. girls

1. What do you see at Zoo #1?

one | two | three | four | five

seven | six | are | is | am

A. Two children are at the zoo.
B. ____ animals ____ at the zoo.
C. ____ adults ____ at the zoo.
D. I ____ not at the zoo.
E. ____ boy ____ at the zoo.
F. ____ girl ____ at the zoo.
G. ____ women ____ at the zoo.
H. ____ people ____ at the zoo.

6C. Activities – Fill in the blanks and find the differences between two pictures.

1. One partner will look at **Zoo picture 1,** and the other partner will look at the following slide, **Zoo Picture 2.** Both partners will fill in the blanks for the correct answers for their own slide picture. They may help each other if needed.

2. Then partner 1 will read their answers aloud to partner 2. Partner 2 will say "Yes, two children are at the zoo." if their answer is the same. Partner 2 will say and write "No, six children are at the zoo." if their answer is different.

3. Then they will switch, and partner 2 will read their answers aloud while partner 1 agrees or disagrees.

Model by giving an example while showing the picture, **"Two children are at the zoo. Yes?"** "Yes, two children are at the zoo."

2. What do you see at Zoo #2?

one		seven
two		six
three		are
four		is
five		am

A. Two children are at the zoo.
B. ___ animals ___ at the zoo.
C. ___ adults ___ at the zoo.
D. I ___ not at the zoo.
E. ___ boy ___ at the zoo.
F. ___ girl ___ at the zoo.
G. ___ women ___ at the zoo.
H. ___ people ___ at the zoo.

©2020-2021 Literacy International

6C. Activities – Fill in the blanks and find the differences between two pictures.

1. One partner will look at **Zoo picture 1,** and the other partner will look at the following slide, **Zoo Picture 2.** Both partners will fill in the blanks for the correct answers for their own slide picture. They may help each other if needed.

2. Then partner 1 will read their answers aloud to partner 2. Partner 2 will agree and say "Yes, two children are at the zoo." if their answer is the same. Partner 2 will say and write "No, six children are at the zoo." if their answer is different.

3. Then they will switch, and partner 2 will read their answers aloud while partner 1 agrees or disagrees.

Model by giving an example while showing the picture, **"Two children are at the zoo. Yes?"** "Yes, two children are at the zoo."

7. Game – 5 minutes

Use paper, a board, or a virtual whiteboard to draw.
Students take turns making simple line drawings of vocabulary words from this lesson and previous lessons. You may give them a list of vocabulary words or flashcards to prompt them. Then other students will guess which words they are. The student that guesses the most words in 5 minutes wins.

1 & 2 Homework

1. Read the next lesson's Bible verse: 1 John 1:5 in your language.

2. Write sentences about your friends and other people. You can use: girl, boy, man, woman, adult, child, I, she, etc.

   A. Mary is a woman. She is an adult.
   B.
   C.
   D.
   E.
   F.

Homework 1, and 2 - Reading the next Bible Lesson in L1, and writing about self with new vocabulary

Students will always read the Bible lesson in their first language (L1) before reading it in English the following lesson. Help them get a Bible in their own language if they don't have one. They may also use Bible.is, ScriptureEarth.org, BibleGateway.com or other Bible translation resources.

Model. Go over each of the homework assignments to be sure the student understands what to do.

Repeat. Encourage students to find someone with whom to practice conversing and reading the completed homework assignment. They may use a bilingual dictionary.

Solo. Students will share their homework when they are finished. Check homework, including spelling. Explain mistakes, and give praise and encouragement. Answers will vary.

3. Write the words for each picture.

1 a child children	2	3	4	5	6
7	8	9	10	11	12

Homework 3 – Write the vocabulary words with the pictures
Number one is an example.

1. a child, children
2. a girl, girls
3. a boy, boys
4. an adult, adults
5. to look, He looks at the phone.
6. a chair, chairs
7. an animal, animals
8. a person, people
9. a man, men
10. a woman, women
11. an enemy, enemies
12. a friend, friends

4. Mark the /oo/ and /ch/ sounds. Then write and say the sentences.

A. I l(oo)k at the good book.	
B. She is a woman.	
C. The child looks at the book.	
D. We are good friends.	
E. They are children.	
F. People sit in (ch)airs at church.	

Homework 4 – Write and say sentences with the new sounds.

This homework practices writing, spelling and pronouncing the /oo/ and /ch/ sounds.

Answers:
  A. I l<u>oo</u>k at the g<u>oo</u>d b<u>oo</u>k.
  B. She is a w<u>o</u>man.
  C. The <u>ch</u>ild l<u>oo</u>ks at the b<u>oo</u>k.
  D. We are g<u>oo</u>d friends.
  E. They are <u>ch</u>ildren.
  F. People sit in <u>ch</u>airs at <u>ch</u>ur<u>ch</u>.

5. Homework – Fill in the blanks.

created   created   children   created   and   and

God ___ the sky ___ the earth. God ___ animals. Last, he ___ people, as man ___ woman, to be like him. He told them to have many ___.

From Genesis 1

Homework 5 – Bible Reading Review

Students may look back at the Bible reading to answer the questions.
Answers:
God <u>created</u> the sky <u>and</u> the earth. God <u>created</u> animals. Last, he <u>created</u> people, as man <u>and</u> woman, to be like him. He told them to have many <u>children</u>.

> ### 6. Homework—Choose 1 Verse to Memorize
>
> **A**
>
> God created the sky and the earth.
>
> Genesis 1:1 ERV
>
> **B**
>
> So God created humans in his own image. He created them to be like himself. He created them male and female.
>
> Genesis 1:27 ERV

Homework 6 – Memorize a Verse

Learners get to choose A, B, or C (on the next slide) to memorize. Please notice that the memory work is not long. Everyone, regardless of skill level, should be able to do it.

1. **Model.** Recite a verse from memory.

2. **Repeat.** Encourage students to find someone with whom to practice conversing and reading the completed homework assignment.

3. **Solo.** Students will recite the verse from memory at the next class.

> # 6. Homework – Choose 1 Verse to Memorize
>
> **C**
>
> My help will come from the Lord, the Creator of heaven and earth.
>
> Psalm 121:2 ERV

Homework 6 – Memorize a Verse

Learners get to choose A, B, (from previous slide) or C to memorize.

7. Homework – Fill in the blanks.

`am` `are` `is` `He` `I` `It` `We` `They` `She` `You`

A. I _____ a person.

B. You _____ an adult.

C. It _____ an animal.

D. She _____ a friend.

E. You _____ enemies.

F. They _____ children.

G. _____ am an adult.

H. _____ is a woman.

I. _____ is a boy.

J. _____ is a man.

K. _____ is a chair.

L. They _____ animals.

Homework 7 – Grammar Review

1. Use the words provided to fill in the blanks of the Bible verses. To model, write "I am a person."

Answers:
A. Am
B. Are
C. Is
D. Is
E. are
F. are
G. I
H. She
I. He
J. He
K. It
L. are

05-30

8. Homework - Fill in the blanks

| are | am | is | Hello | is | Goodbye |

To: Jake@Jmail.org

Subject: The beach is good!

___1___ Jake,

I ___2___ at the beach with friends. The water ___3___ good. The food and drinks ___4___ good. My chair ___5___ good. We play ball. People smile and say hello. The children love the water.

___6___
Liz

Homework 8. Everyday reading and writing

The learners will read the email and fill in the blanks.

Answers:
1. Hello
2. am
3. is
4. are
5. is
6. Goodbye

05-31

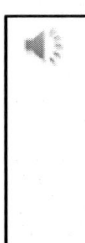

9. Homework - Now I Can...

- ☐ I can understand I, you, he, she, it, we and they.
- ☐ I can read, write, say, and understand the 12 vocabulary words.
- ☐ I understand opposites.
- ☐ I understand that God is our Creator.

Homework 9 – I can statements checklist.

The student must be able to achieve all of these skills before the next lesson. If not, the lesson can be repeated.
Review all of the skills at the beginning of the next lesson. Be sure to give lots of praise and encouragement!

Closing Prayer

Pray

You may want to ask for any special prayer requests, then pray for your students and bless them.

Light of the World
Learning English through the Bible
Lesson A1-06

©2020-2021 Literacy International

Teacher's Notes:

Bible Reading: God is light - 1 John 1:5
Theme: Polite Language: Please, thank you, you're welcome
Pronunciation: /aw/ and /u/ schwa
Grammar: am, is, are, pronouns
Preparation:
- Pray
- Read 1 John 1:5
- Preview slides and game
- Optional: Bring a light to turn on and off, play money, school and office supplies

Pray, Review, and Preview

Bible Reading: God is light - 1 John 1:5
Theme: Polite Language: Please, thank you, you're welcome
Pronunciation: /u/ schwa and /aw/
Grammar:
- am, is, are,
- pronouns

©2020-2021 Literacy International

Pray

Pray for the class. You may want to thank the Lord for people who help us.

Check Homework and Review

Ask each student to read aloud or recite their homework from the last class. Check written work. Be sure they have read 1 John 1:5 in their native languages in preparation for the lesson.

Review the main points of the previous lesson, and ask if there are any questions.

What do you see?

1A. Discuss Theme Picture

- Ask "What do you see in this picture?" and "What else?" to elicit vocabulary they already know.
- Repeat and write their words or show the words on the next slide.

Answers may include: people, man, woman, boy, girl, children, please, thank you, sorry, etc.

More advanced students can be encouraged to make complete sentences:
Thank you for your help. The girl says, "I'm sorry."

What do you see?

- Thank you.
- You're welcome.
- That's okay. No problem.
- I'm sorry!
- Happy birthday!
- Thank you!

1B. Show Words for Theme Picture

Please show the names of the theme picture items to the students briefly.
These words can be studied for homework.
Practice of vocabulary begins with the following slide.

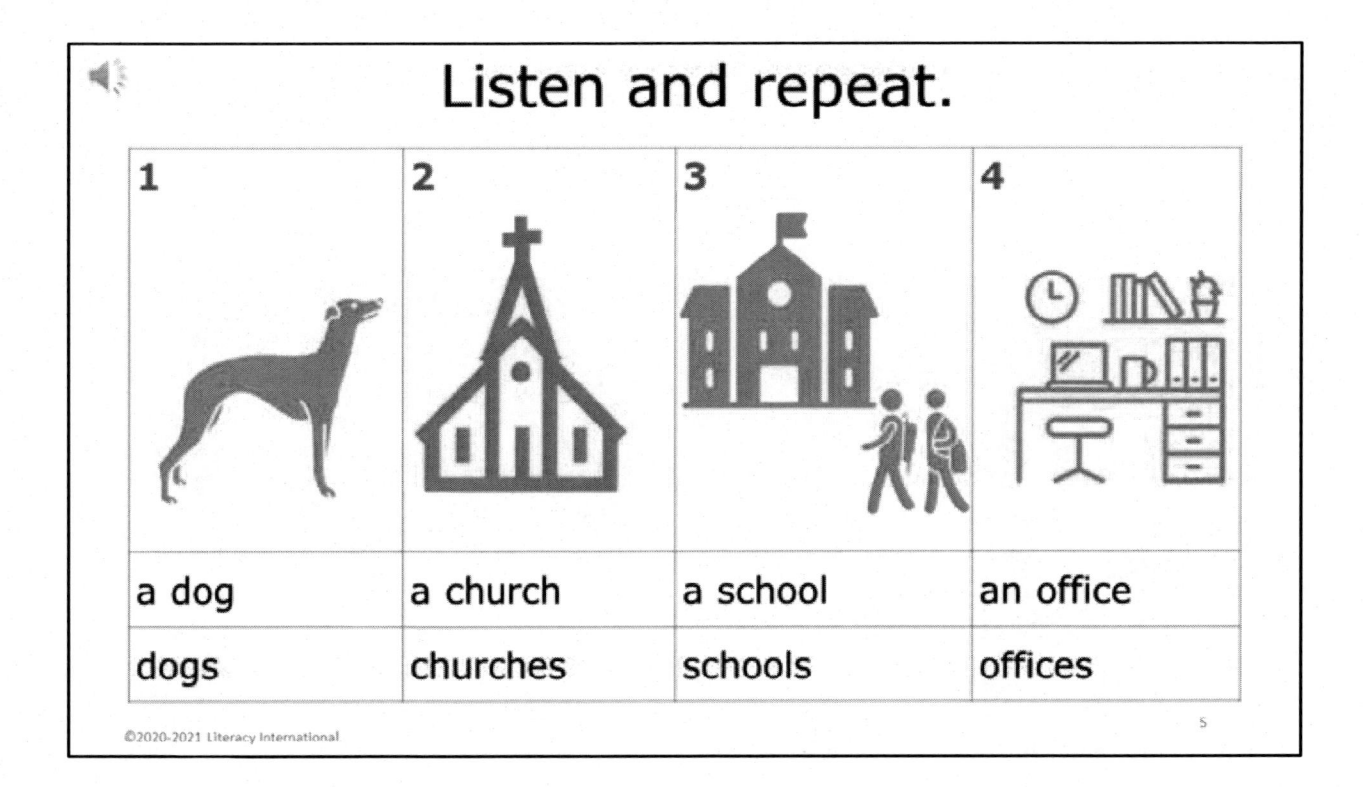

1	2	3	4
a dog	a church	a school	an office
dogs	churches	schools	offices

Listen and repeat.

2A. Vocabulary

1. **Say the new words in a simple sentence, such as** "This is a dog," several times, while indicating the object or picture. Students just watch and listen. Be sure to use a natural speaking voice and good rhythm and intonation.

2. **Say the word and the article that goes with it several times**, as you indicate the object. For example, say: *a dog, a dog, a dog*. Have your students then repeat the word after you several times.

3. **Say the word in the same sentence again**. Have students repeat after you each time, "This is a dog."

4. **Check students' comprehension by asking direct questions**. For example, *What is this? Where's the church? Is this an office?*

Listen and repeat.

5	6	7	8
the world	money	light	dark/darkness
worlds			

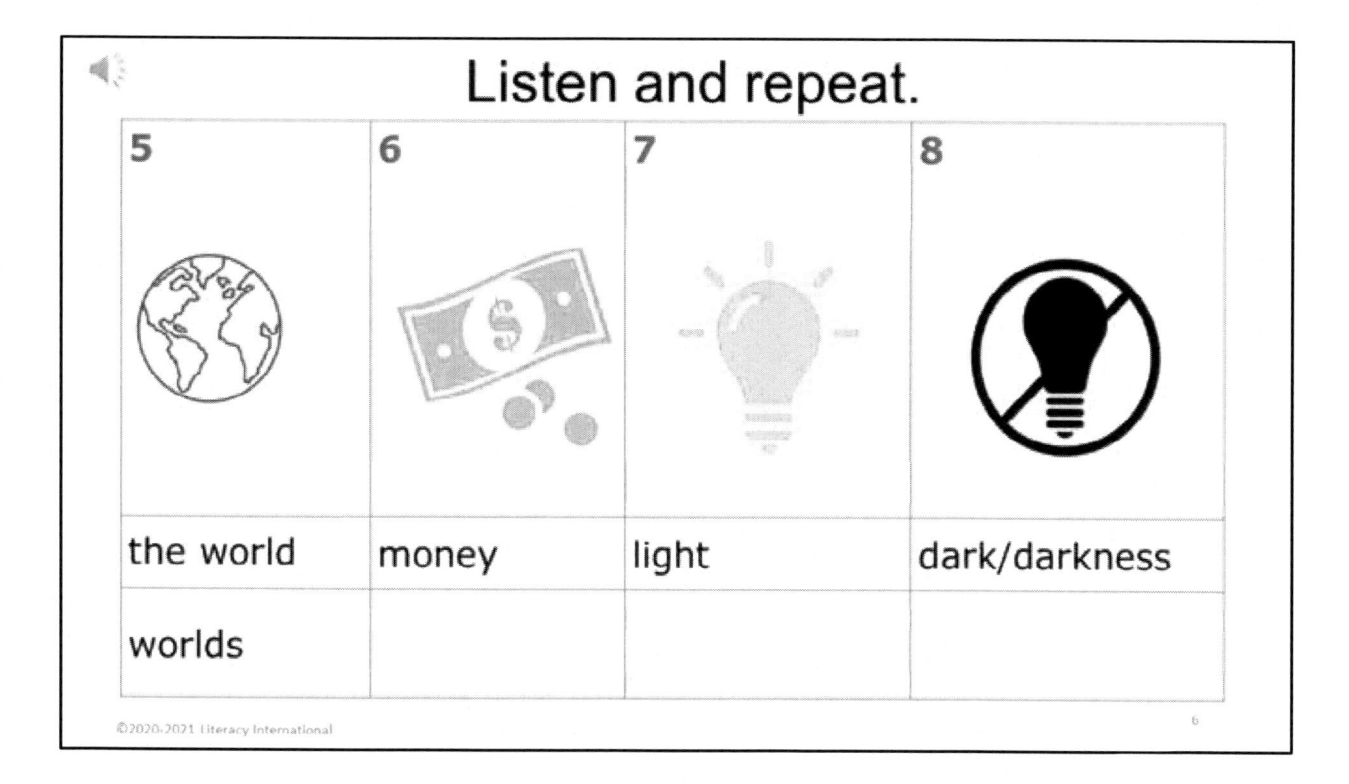

2B. Vocabulary

1. **Say the new words in a simple sentence, such as** "This is the world," several times, while indicating the object or picture. Students just watch and listen. Be sure to use a natural speaking voice and good rhythm and intonation.

2. **Say the word and the article that goes with it several times**, as you indicate the object. For example, say: *the world, the world, the world*. Have your students then repeat the word after you several times.

3. **Say the word in the same sentence again**. Have students repeat after you each time, "This is the world."

4. **Check students' comprehension by asking direct questions**. For example, *What is this? Where's the money? Is this light?*

9	10	11	12
to turn on	to turn off	to lose	to find
Please turn on the light.	Please turn off the light.	He lost a sheep.	He found the sheep.

Listen and repeat.

2C. Vocabulary

1. **Say the new words in a simple sentence, such as** "This is to turn on," several times, while indicating the object or picture. Students just watch and listen. Be sure to use a natural speaking voice and good rhythm and intonation.

2. **Say the word and the article that goes with it several times**, as you indicate the object. For example, say: *to turn on, to turn on, to turn on*. Have your students then repeat the word after you several times.

3. **Say the word in the same sentence again.** Have students repeat after you each time, "This is to turn on."

4. **Check students' comprehension by asking direct questions**. For example, *What is this? Who lost a sheep? Who found the sheep?*

Listen and repeat.

Pronoun	To Be	Contraction	Negative -	Question ?
I	am	I'm	I'm not	Am I?
he she it	is	he's she's it's	he's not she's not it's not	Is he? Is she? Is it?
you we they	are	you're we're they're	you're not we're not they're not	Are you? Are we? Are they?

1. You're welcome.
2. I'm sorry.

2D. Grammar

Spoken English usually uses the contraction forms. Written English uses the full forms.
Note that the blue letters are replaced by apostrophes to form the contractions.

Model, Repeat, and Solo the pronunciation of all forms shown on the chart.

Describe with you're, he's, she's, it's, they're.

2E. Grammar and Vocabulary Practice

Students describe the pictures with simple sentences using contractions.

Answers may include:
1. It's a dog.
2. He's in a chair.
3. They're at the beach
4. He's lost.
5. They're at the office.
6. It's found. He found money.
7. It's the world.
8. They're happy.

> ## Listen and repeat.
>
> A: Oh no! I lost some money. I need to find it
>
> B: It's okay. I can help you look.
>
> A: Thank you!
>
> B: You're welcome. Is it at school?
>
> A: Maybe. Let's look!

3A. Conversation 1

1. **Model: Say both parts of the conversation several times.** Use A and B cards, stick figures, or change your physical position to indicate the dual parts. Role-play the parts to convey the meaning of the conversation. **Students watch and listen.**

2. **Repeat: Say one line at a time and have students repeat until they can be understood.**

3. **Solo: You begin the conversation and call on individual students to respond.** Then reverse the roles (students are A, you are B).

4. Once students can do both parts, **encourage free conversation** (students substitute the blue words for other lost things: **phone, pen, dog, notebook,** etc.)

> # Listen and repeat.
>
> A: Can you please **turn off the music**?
>
> B: Sure, no problem.
>
> A. Can you please **turn on the light**? Thank you.
>
> B: You're welcome.

3B. Conversation 2

1. Model: Say both parts of the conversation several times. Use A and B cards, stick figures, or change your physical position to indicate the dual parts. Role-play the parts to convey the meaning of the conversation. **Students just watch and listen.**

2. **Repeat: Say one line at a time and have students repeat until they can be understood.**

3. **Solo: You begin the conversation and call on individual students to respond.** Then reverse the roles (students are A, you are B).

4. Once students can do both parts, **encourage free conversation** substituting their own words for the blue words **(find, turn on, turn off, phone, faucet, TV, etc.).**

Listen and repeat.

1. /u/	2. /aw/	3. Challenge
sun	lost	
run	dog	
one	off	
money	office	
up	faucet	

A. I lost my dog and my money.
B. Please turn off the faucet.

©2020-2021 Literacy International

4A. Pronunciation - Sound and Spelling

1. **Model: Say the sound several times while pointing to it.** (For example, point to the **u** and say /u/ /u/ /u/. **Then say the sound and quickly read the entire list, pointing to each item as you read it** (/u/ sun, run, one, money, up). Students just watch and listen.

2. **Repeat: Say the sound and each word several times, having students repeat each time after you in unison.** Be sure to use your normal voice and rate of speed. Do one column at a time, top to bottom. Then read the sentences below the chart.

3. **Solo: Call on individuals to say a sound and its word group.** Give lots of praise.

4. **Challenge:** Choose another sound from the lesson that is challenging for your particular students to pronounce. Use words

from Parts 1 and 2 of the lesson and from previous lessons to make a group of 3-5 words. You may repeat the same challenging sounds in several lessons. Students need a lot of practice on sounds that do not exist in their first language.

Listen and repeat.

A. —	B. — -	C. — - -
light	office	It's a dog.
dark	faucet	I'm a man.
school	money	She's a girl.
church	welcome	They are friends.

4B. Hum and clap the stress.

Begin by humming the stress of a column of words. Hum higher, longer, and louder for big dashes and lower, shorter, and quieter for small dashes.

You may use hand gestures to indicate that **the stressed syllable is higher in pitch, longer in duration and louder.** Invite your students to join in humming the rhythm. Once the class is humming the rhythm in unison, you can begin saying the words. You may also wish to clap the syllables while you say the words.

1. Model: Hum and then say each word in the group several times. Students listen.
2. Repeat: Students repeat words after you in unison.
3. Solo: Call on individuals to read the entire group of words.

God is light
1 John 1:5

We heard the true teaching from God. Now we tell it to you: God is light, and in him there is no darkness. ERV

©2020-2021 Literacy International

5. Bible Reading

Students have already read this story in their native language as part of their homework, so it will be familiar even if they do not know all the vocabulary yet. The pictures also help them to understand. The hyperlink of the Bible verses will take you to https://live.bible.is/ where you can select from over 1,000 languages to read and listen to the verses.

A. Read the verse out loud to the class.
B. Give simple definitions for words students ask about.
C. Ask for volunteers to read aloud.
D. Ask if there are any questions or comments about the story.
E. Ask question: Who is light? Who is in the picture?

Listen and write one word per line.

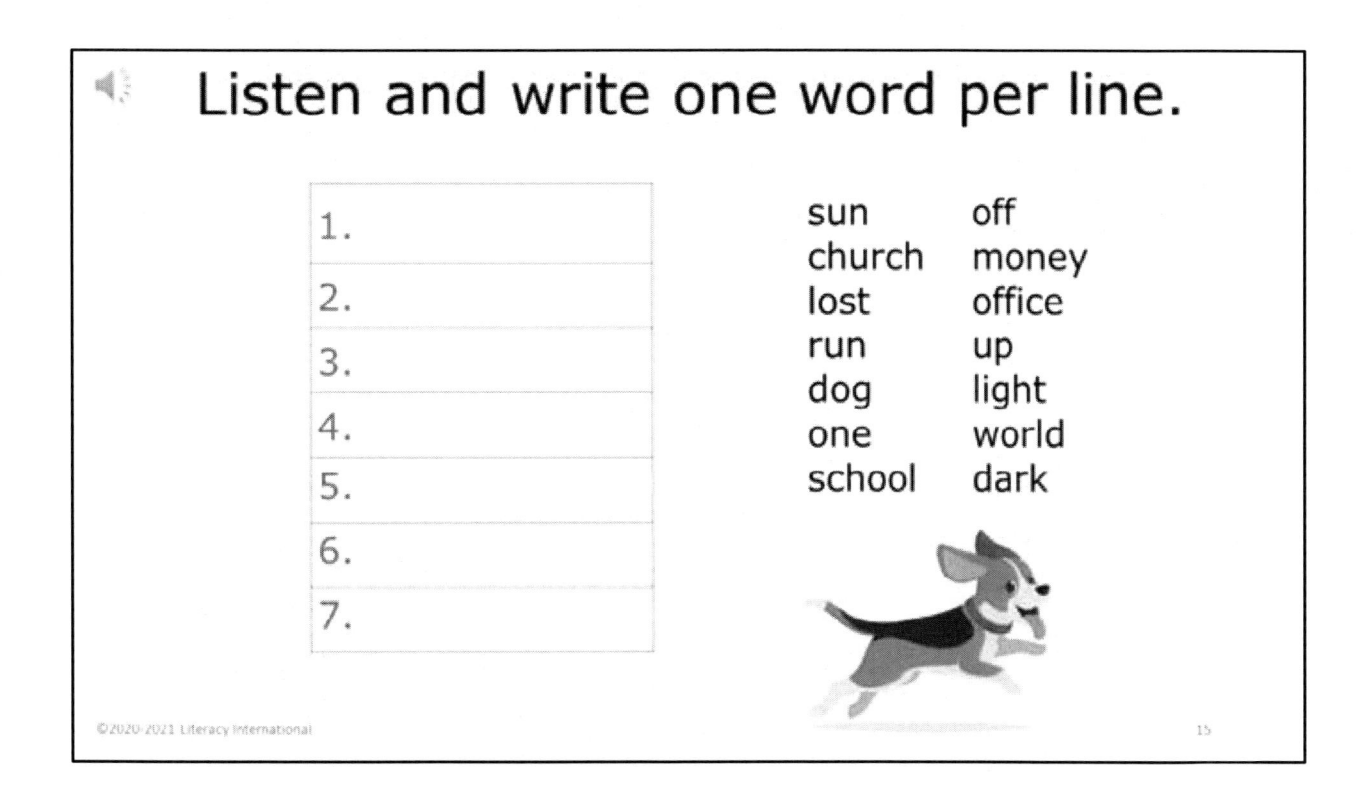

1.
2.
3.
4.
5.
6.
7.

sun   off
church   money
lost   office
run   up
dog   light
one   world
school   dark

6A. Activities - Dictation of sound/spelling words

Read the words with a sample sentence and have students write just one word for each line. Check spelling.

For more advanced students, you can hide the sample word bank.

1. office, office (I'm in my office.) office
2. up, up (Get up!) up
3. one, one (I have one child.) one
4. off, off (Please turn off the light.) off
5. run, run (He likes to run.) run
6. dog, dog (This is a dog.) dog
7. money, money (It's my money.) money

Listen and circle the words you hear.

Questions	
1. **(turn on)**/turn off	8. sorry/school
2. Please/She's	9. okay/say
3. find/lose	10. light/father
4. thanks/thank you	11. darkness/welcome
5. we're/you're	12. off/on
6. school/church	13. birthdate/church
7. light/lost	14. lose/you

6B. Activities – Listening

Students listen and circle the the words they hear.

Answers:
1. Please turn on the faucet.
2. Please turn off the light.
3. I'm sorry to lose the money.
4. Thank you for the office chair.
5. You're welcome. It's no problem.
6. I lost my notebook at school.
7. Did you find your lost dog?
8. I'm sorry I'm not at school.
9. No problem. It's okay.
10. God is light.
11. Darkness isn't in him.
12. The office is dark. Please turn on the lights.
13. It's my church.
14. Happy birthday to you!

Describe the pictures

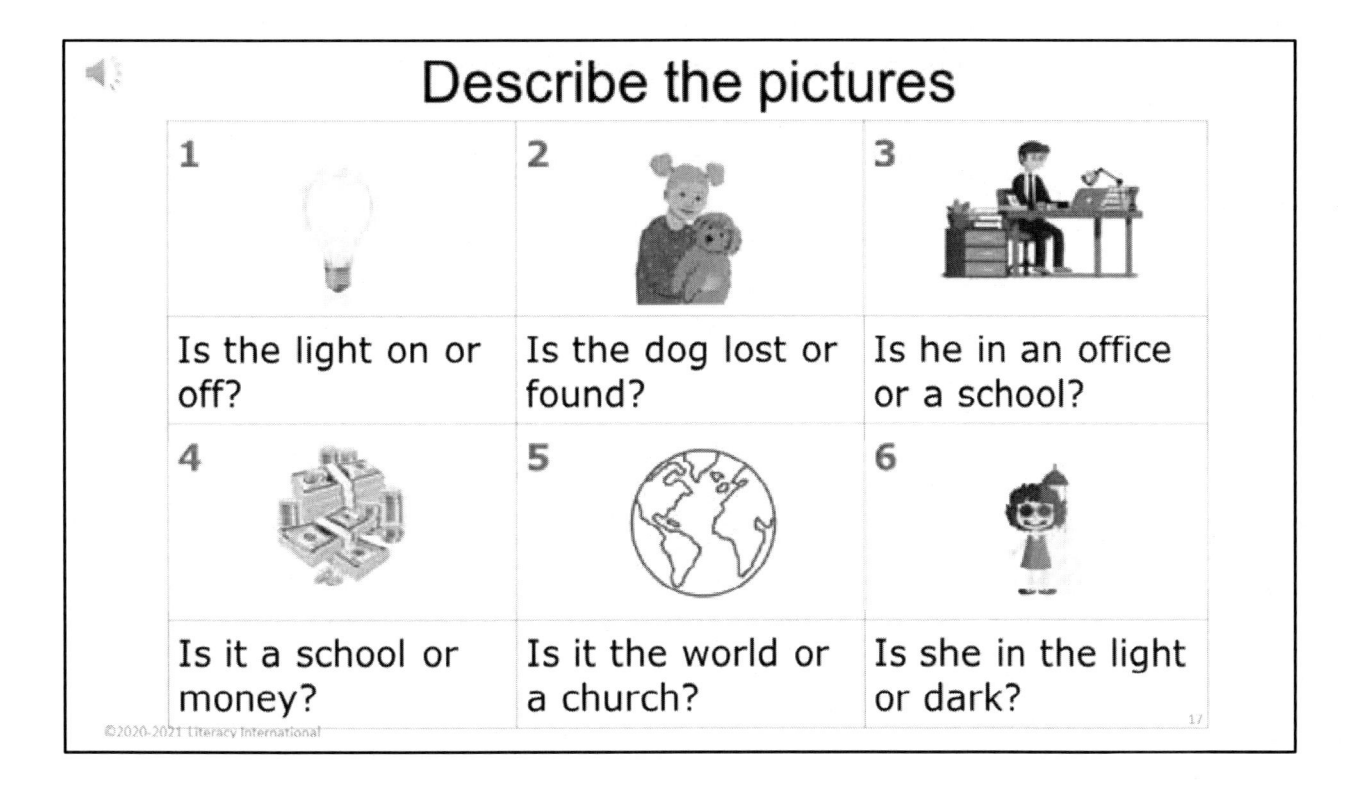

1	2	3
Is the light on or off?	Is the dog lost or found?	Is he in an office or a school?
4	5	6
Is it a school or money?	Is it the world or a church?	Is she in the light or dark?

6C. Activities - Pair work.

Ask the students to describe a picture to their partner with a sentence. Partner A must ask the question and write the answer given in a sentence.

Then switch, and partner B must ask the question and write the answer given in a sentence.

Model by giving an example, "Is the light on? "The light is on." Or "It is on."

Game - Charades

Act out the vocabulary words.

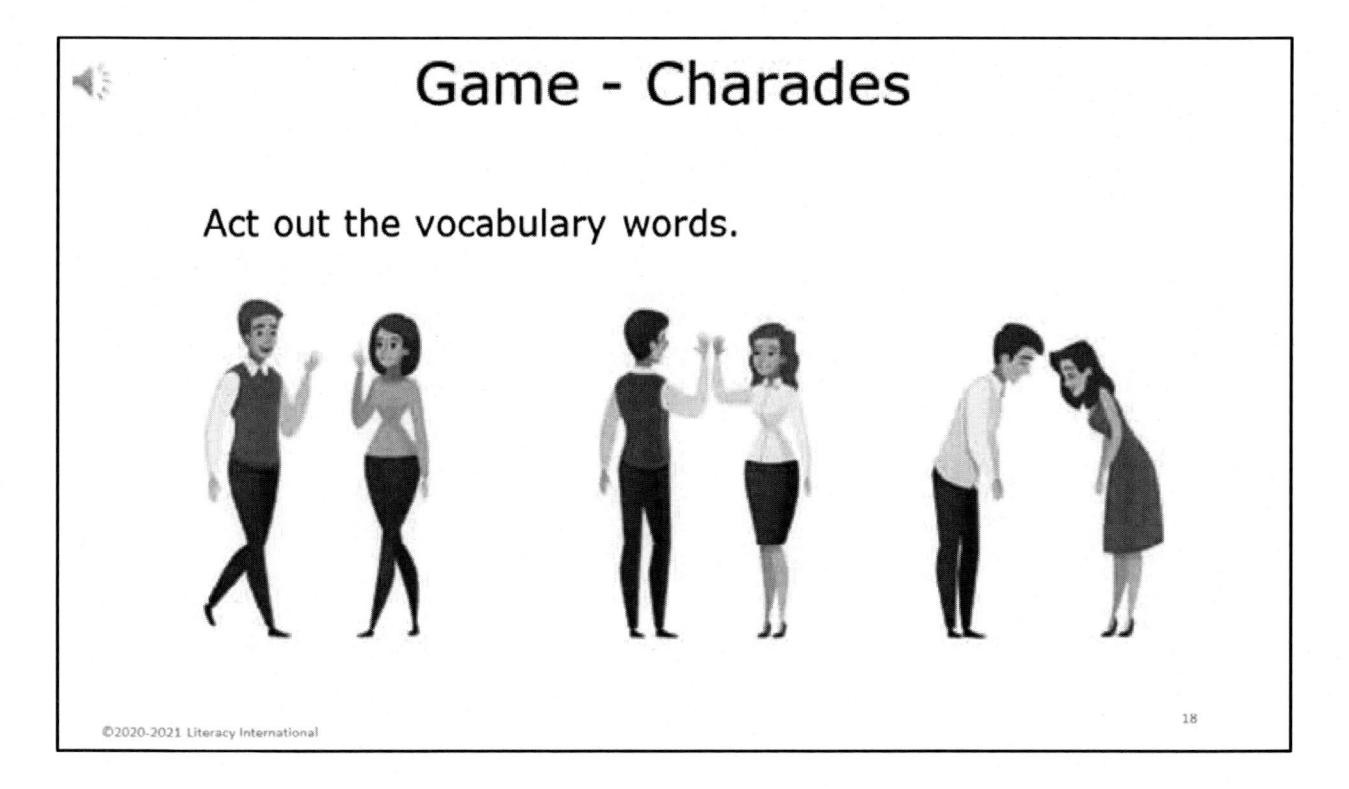

7. Game

Charades: Each student takes turns acting out various vocabulary words from the list of previous vocabulary (see appendix for list). The person who guesses the most correctly is the winner.

Give each student a sheet of paper with 5 different vocabulary words selected from this lesson and previous lessons. If you are teaching online, use the chat feature to send different vocabulary words to each student.

1. Model: Act out each of the vocabulary words: **lose, find, dog, turn on, turn off,** etc. and have the students guess the word.

2. Repeat: have the students do the acting out gestures with you

3. Solo: Have the students act out the words and guess what the words are.

> # 1 & 2 Homework
>
> 1. Read the next lesson's Bible verses: Genesis 1:1–2:25 in your language.
>
> 2. Write 6 sentences with contractions. Use: I'm, you're, he's, she's, it's, we're, they're.
>
> A. He's lost. It's dark.
> B.
> C.
> D.
> E.
> F.
> G.

Homework 1, and 2 - Reading the next Bible Lesson in L1 and writing about self with new vocabulary

Students will always read the Bible lesson in their first language (L1) before reading it in English the following lesson. Help them get a Bible in their own language if they don't have one. They may also use Bible.is, ScriptureEarth.org, or other Bible translation resources. The hyperlink of the Bible verses connects to https://live.bible.is where students can select from over 1,000 languages to read and listen to the verses.

Model. Go over each of the homework assignments to be sure the student understands what to do.

Repeat. Encourage students to find someone with whom to practice conversing and reading the completed homework assignment. They may use a bilingual dictionary.

Solo. Students will share their homework when they are finished. After they have shared their homework, be sure to check it for correctness, including spelling. Explain mistakes, while providing praise and encouragement. Answers will vary.

3. Write the words for each picture.

1 🐕	2	3 💡	4 🌍	5	6
a dog					
dogs					
7 🏫	8 ⛪	9	10 💵	11	12

©2020-2021 Literacy International

20

Homework 3 – Write the vocabulary words with the pictures
Number one is an example.

Answers:
1. a dog, dogs
2. an office, offices
3. light
4. the world, worlds
5. to lose, He lost a sheep.
6. to find, He found the sheep.
7. a school, schools
8. a church, churches
9. dark
10. money
11. to turn on, Please turn on the light.
12. to turn off, Please turn off the lights.

06-20

4. Write and say the sentences

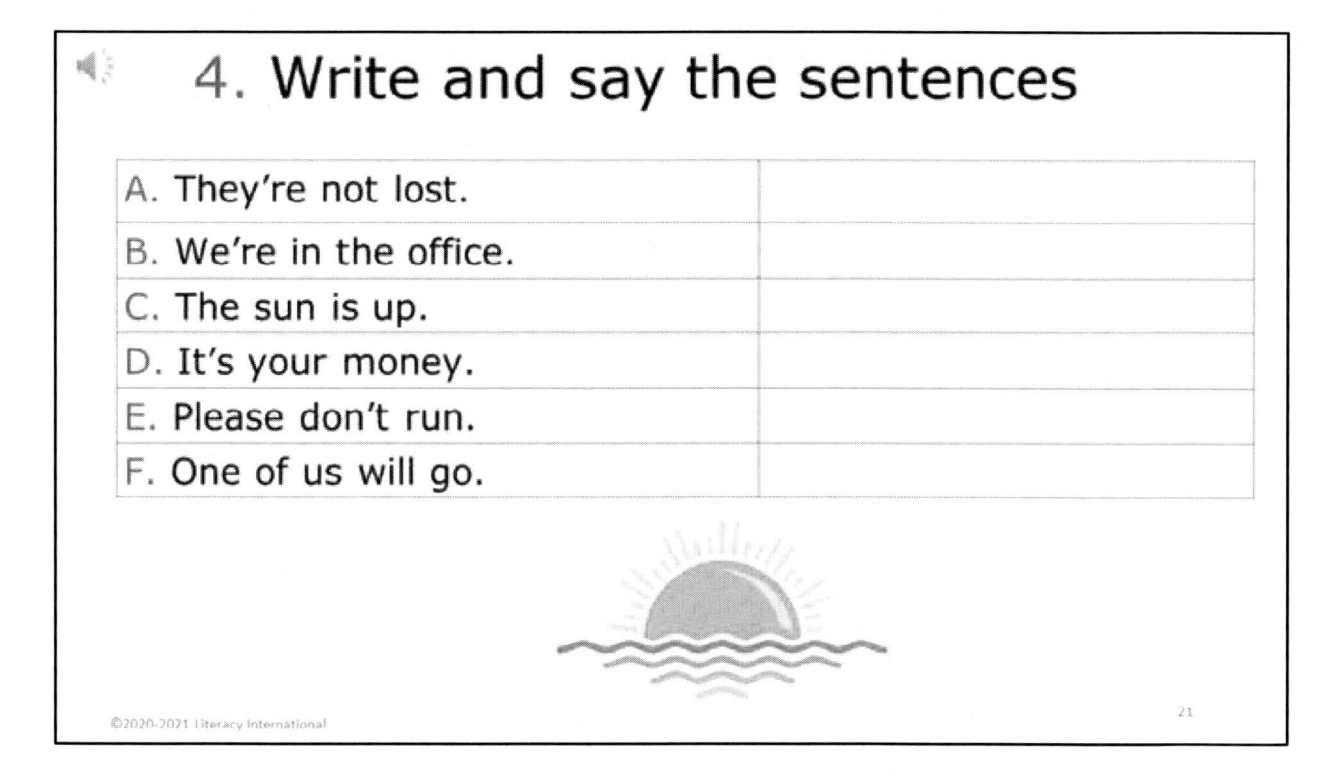

A. They're not lost.	
B. We're in the office.	
C. The sun is up.	
D. It's your money.	
E. Please don't run.	
F. One of us will go.	

Homework 4 – Write and say sentences with the new sounds.

This homework practices writing, spelling, and pronouncing the /u/ and /aw/ sounds.

5. Homework

Fill in the blanks.

light **you** **darkness** **we**

We heard the true teaching from God. Now ____ tell it to ____: God is ____, and in him there is no ____.

1 John 1:5 ERV

Homework 5 – Bible Story Review

Fill in the blanks.
We heard the true teaching from God. Now we tell it to you: God is light, and in him there is no darkness.

> # 6. Homework – Choose 1 Verse to Memorize
>
> **A**
>
> We heard the true teaching from God. Now we tell it to you: God is light, and in him there is no darkness.
> 1 John 1:5 ERV
>
> **B**
>
> The light shines in the darkness, and the darkness has not defeated it.
> John 1:5 ERV

Homework 6 – Memorize a Verse

Learners get to choose A, B, or C (on the next slide) to memorize. Please notice that the memory work is not long. Everyone, regardless of skill level, should be able to do it.

1. **Model.** Recite a verse from memory.

2. **Repeat.** Encourage students to find someone with whom to practice conversing and reading the completed homework assignment.

3. **Solo.** Students will recite the verse from memory at the next class.

> # 6. Homework – Choose 1 Verse to Memorize
>
> **C**
>
> Later, Jesus talked to the people again. He said, "I am the light of the world. Whoever follows me will never live in darkness. They will have the light that gives life."
> John 8:12 ERV

Homework 6 – Memorize a Verse

Learners get to choose A, B, (from previous slide) or C to memorize.

7. Homework

They're   We're   it's   She's   I'm   You're   He's

A. Jesus said, "I am (_____) the light of the world."

B. He is (_____) a friend of God.

C. We are (_____) the church of God.

D. You are (_____) our God.

E. She is (_____) a child of God.

F. They are (_____) good people.

©2020-2021 Literacy International

Homework 7 – Grammar Review

Use the contractions to fill in the blanks of the Bible verses.

Answers:
A. I'm
John 8:12
B. He's
John 15:14
C. We're
1 Corinthians 3:16
D. You're
Jeremiah 3:22
E. She's
Romans 8:14
F. They're
Proverbs 19:17

8. Homework

A. What is lost?
B. What is its name?
C. What color is it?
D. What is the phone number?
E. How much money is the reward?
F. What date was the dog lost?

Lost Dog! Please help find Dawn. $50 Reward.

Dawn is a dark colored dog lost on August 8. Please call 312-987-5555 if you find Dawn. Thank you!

Homework 8 – Everyday Reading and Writing.

The learners will read and answer the questions.

Answers:
- A. A dog.
- B. Dawn
- C. Dark colored
- D. 312-987-5555
- E. $50
- F. August 8

9. Homework - Write sentences

What is your name, **please**?			
1. please	2. thank you	3. turn off	4. you're welcome
5. church	6. school	7. I'm sorry	8. no problem

Homework 9 – Writing about theme or Bible Story

Model. Write a sentence using the phrases.

10. Homework - Now I Can...

☐ I can understand I'm, you're, he's, she's, it's, we're, they're.

☐ I can read, write, say, and understand the 12 vocabulary words.

☐ I can say please, thank you, you're welcome, I'm sorry, that's okay, no problem.

Homework 10 – I can statements checklist.

The student must be able to achieve all of these skills before the next lesson. If not, the lesson can be repeated.
Review all of the skills at the beginning of the next lesson. Give lots of praise and encouragement!

Closing Prayer

Pray
You may want to ask for any special prayer requests, then pray for your students and bless them.

Light of the World

Learning English through the Bible
Lesson A1-07
©2020-2021 Literacy International

Teacher's Notes:
Bible Readings: God is love. God loves you. God is our father. God is good. God is our creator. God is light.
Themes: Alphabet & Numbers, Nice to meet you! Basic needs, Personal information, People, Polite language
Pronunciation: /A/ /E/ /a/ /yU/ /A/ /b/ /d/ /n/ /oo/ /ch/ /aw/ /u/
Grammar:
- Spell name and say phone number
- Nice to meet you. How are you?
- I need…
- What's your __? my, your, his, her
- Am/is/are
- Subject pronouns

Preparation:
- Pray
- Preview slides and songs
- Optional: Bring objects related to the lessons

Pray, Review, and Preview

Bible Readings:
- God is love.
- God loves you.
- God is our father.
- God is good.
- God is our creator.
- God is light.

Themes:
- Alphabet & Numbers
- Nice to meet you!
- Basic needs
- Personal information
- People
- Polite language

Pray

Pray for the class and thank the Lord for the progress they are making in learning English and the Bible.

Check Homework and Review

Ask each student to read aloud or recite their homework from the last class. Check written work. Review the main points of the previous lesson and ask if there are any questions.

Preview

Pronunciation:

- /A/ and /E/
- /a/ and /yU/
- /A/ and /b/
- /d/ and /n/
- /oo/ and /ch/
- /aw/ and /u/

Grammar:

- Spell name and say phone number
- Nice to meet you. How are you?
- I need...
- What's your ___? my, your, his, her
- Am/is/are
- Subject pronouns

©2020-2021 Literacy International

These are all the sounds and grammar points that will be covered in this lesson.

What do you see?

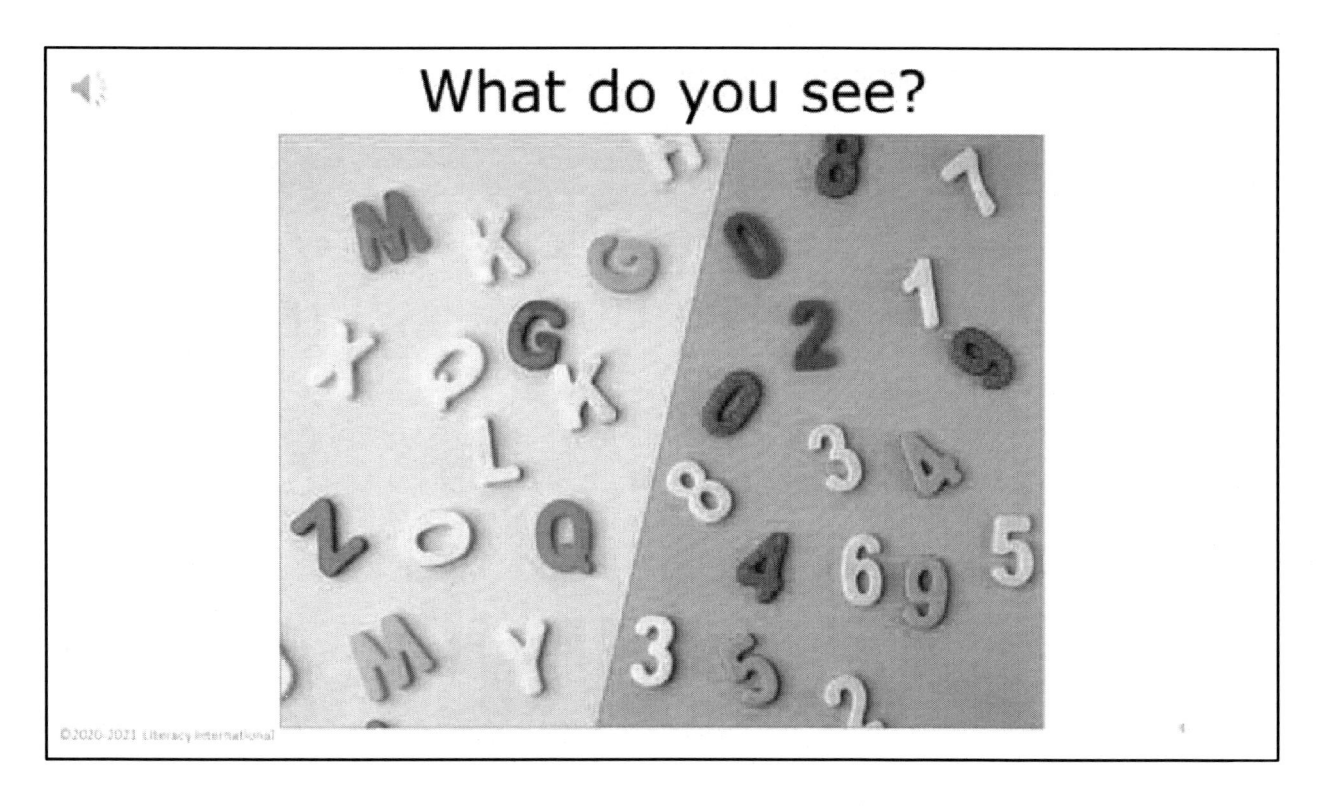

1A. Discuss Theme Picture

- Ask "What do you see in this picture?" and "What else?" to elicit vocabulary they already know.
- Repeat their answers.
- Use English only as much as possible.

Answers may include: letters, numbers, alphabet, M, K, 3, 4, etc.

More advanced students can be encouraged to make complete sentences:
"There are many letters. The number 3 is yellow."

1B. Discuss Theme Picture

- Ask "What do you see in this picture?" and "What else?" to elicit vocabulary they already know.
- Repeat their answers.
- Answers may include: people, wave, hug, handshake, etc.

More advanced students can be encouraged to make complete sentences:
"The men say hello. They shake hands."

1C. Discuss Theme Picture

- Ask "What do you see in this picture?" and "What else?" to elicit vocabulary they already know.
- Repeat their answers.

Answers may include: bottle, water, drink, eat, fork, spoon, plate, glass, cup, table, chair, people, food, etc.

More advanced students can be encouraged to make complete sentences:
They eat at the table.

What do you see?

DRIVER LICENSE
DOB 01/01/1984
EXPIRES 01/01/2020 CLASS C
FN Ben MN James   SEX M
LN Green   HGT 5'-8"
489 Good St.   HAIR BRN
Chicago, IL   WGT 184 lb
60987   EYES BLU
DL F28938203

Registration Form
First Name: Noah
Middle Name: Dan
Last Name: Lee
Email: Lee@Dmail.com
Phone Number: 217-555-1234
Birth Date: 06/09/1999
Address: 123 New St. Newton, NY 23574
Languages: French, English, Ga
Photo:

©2020-2021 Literacy International

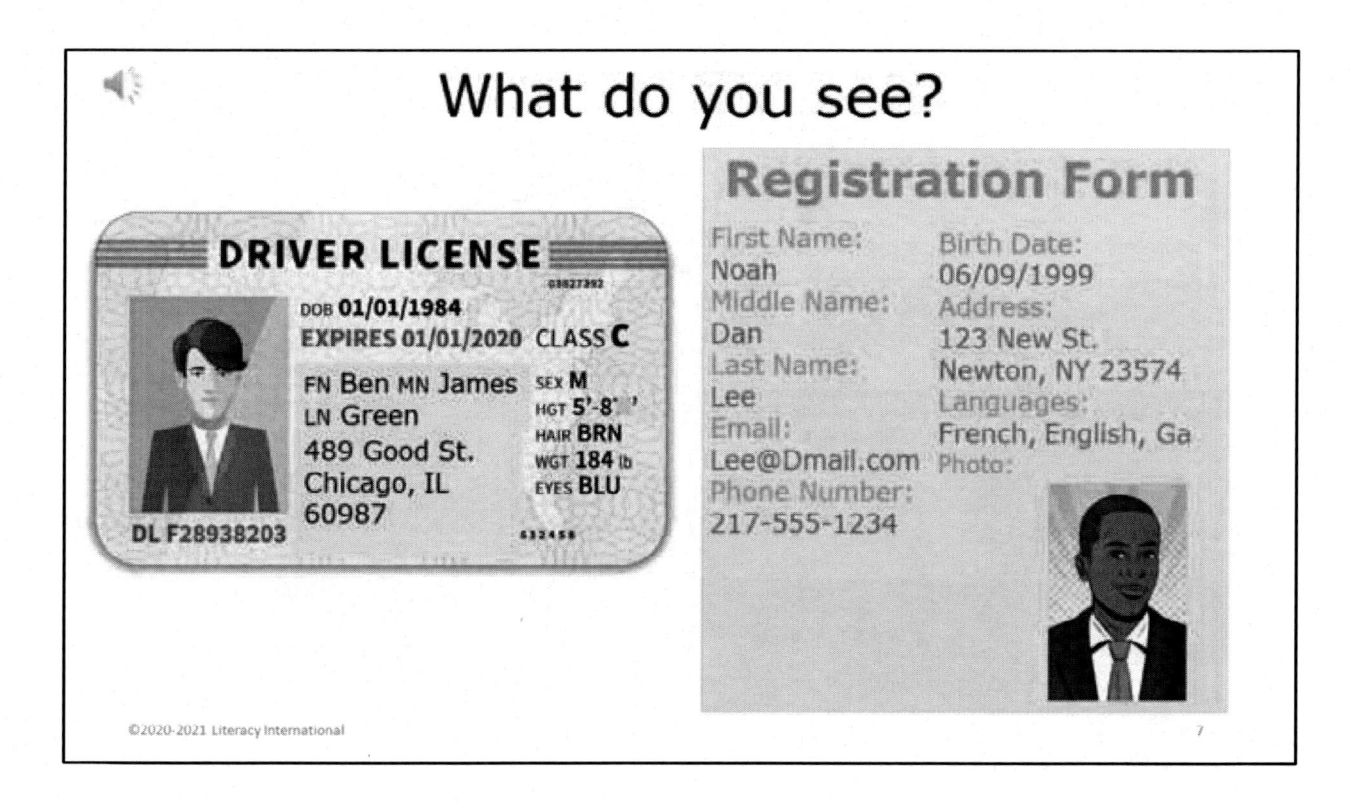

1D. Discuss Theme Picture

- Ask "What do you see in this picture?" and "What else?" to elicit vocabulary they already know.
- Repeat their answers.

Answers may include: name, email, address, ID card, etc.

More advanced students can be encouraged to make complete sentences:
This is a registration form for Noah Lee.

What do you see?

1E. Discuss Theme Picture

- Ask "What do you see in this picture?" and "What else?" to elicit vocabulary they already know.
- Repeat their answers.

Answers may include: **people, man, woman, girl, boy, children, animal**
More advanced students can be encouraged to make complete sentences:
This is a man. This is a woman. These are children. There are two boys and three girls.

1F. Discuss Theme Picture

- Ask "What do you see in this picture?" and "What else?" to elicit vocabulary they already know.
- Repeat their answers.

Answers may include: **people, man, woman, boy, girl, children, please, thank you, you're welcome, sorry, that's okay, no problem,** etc.

More advanced students can be encouraged to make complete sentences:
Thank you for your help. The girl says, "I'm sorry."

> **Listen and repeat.**
>
> 1. Please spell your name.
> 2. What is your phone number?
>
> Adam   Eve
> Abe   Sara
> David Abigail

2A. Grammar

Model, Repeat, and Solo the pronunciation of these phrases.

Demonstrate spelling your name and giving your phone number to the class.
You may also spell the names on your students' nametags and/or the nametags in the picture.

Listen and repeat.

	Phrase	Response
1.	Hello, how are you?	I'm good, thanks. I'm fine, thank you.
2.	Nice to meet you!	Nice to meet you, too.
3.	Hi, my name is ___.	Hi, my name is ___.
4.	What is your name?	My name is ___.
5.	Goodbye.	Goodbye.

2B. Grammar – Simple greetings and phrases.

Model, Repeat, and Solo the pronunciation of all phrases shown on the chart.

You can explain that in informal speech people say "hi" and "I'm good," while in formal speech they say "hello" and "I am fine." Both are acceptable.

Listen and repeat.

I need _____.

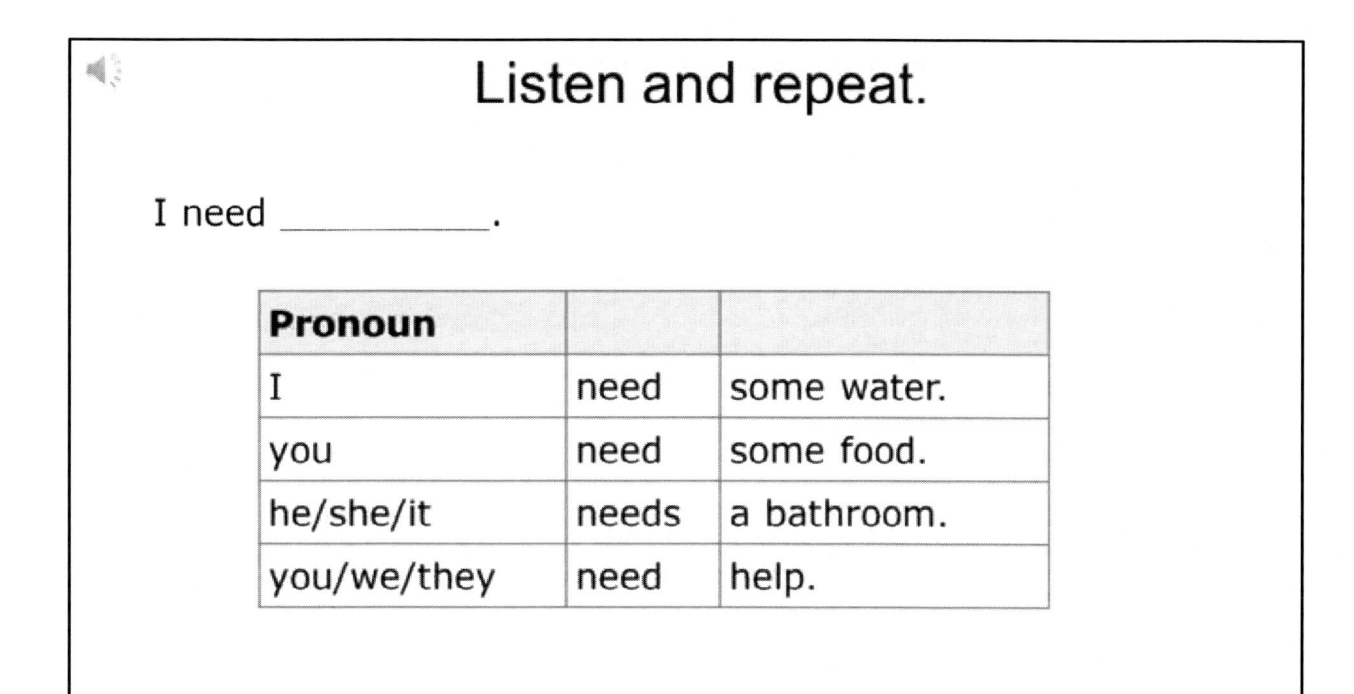

Pronoun		
I	need	some water.
you	need	some food.
he/she/it	needs	a bathroom.
you/we/they	need	help.

2C. Grammar

Model, Repeat, and Solo the pronunciation of all forms shown on the chart.

> ## Listen and repeat.
>
> | Question ? | | Answer |
> |---|---|---|
> | What is your
What's your | name?
address?
phone number?
birthdate?
email?
first language? | Sara Smith
321 Green Street, London
708-487-9870
May 1, 1999
Sara@Dmail.com
French |

2D. Grammar

Spoken English usually uses the contraction forms. Written English usually uses the full forms.

Model, Repeat, and Solo the pronunciation of all forms shown on the chart.

Listen and repeat.

Possessive Adjective	Sentence
1. my	My name is ___.
2. your	Your name is ___.
3. his	His name is Adam.
4. her	Her name is Sara.

2E. Grammar

Model, Repeat, and Solo the pronunciation of all forms shown on the chart.

Model: Gesture to yourself for "My name is ___" and gesture to your student for "Your name is ___."
Point to the man for "his" and to the woman for "her."

Repeat: Have the student repeat the sentences but be sure they use their own name for 1 and your name for 2.

Solo: The student reads all sentences alone.

Listen and repeat.

	Pronoun	To Be	Sentence
Singular 1	I	am	I am a person.
	you	are	You are a person.
	he she it	is	He is a man. She is a woman. It is an animal.
Plural 2+	we you they	are	We are people. You are people. They are people.

2F. Grammar: Subject Pronouns and Am, Is, Are

Note:
- **Pronouns** replace a noun when the subject is already known.
- **They** can refer to people or objects.

Model, Repeat, and Solo the pronunciation of all forms shown on the chart. Discuss the sentences given as examples.

Listen and repeat.

Pronoun	To Be	Contraction	Negative -	Question ?
I	am	I'm	I'm not	Am I?
he she it	is	he's she's it's	he's not she's not it's not	Is he? Is she? Is it?
you we they	are	you're we're they're	you're not we're not they're not	Are you? Are we? Are they?

1. You're welcome.
2. I'm sorry.

2G. Grammar

Spoken English usually uses the contraction forms. Written English usually uses the full forms.
Note that the blue letters are replaced by apostrophes to form the contractions.

Model, Repeat, and Solo the pronunciation of all forms shown on the chart.

> ## Conversation Questions A
>
> 1. What's your phone number?
> 2. Please spell your name.
> 3. How are you?
> 4. Nice to meet you.
> 5. What do you need?
> 6. How is she? ➡

3A. Conversation Practice – Pair work

With a partner, students will practice asking and answering the questions.

Answers will vary.

6. She is fine. or, She is good.

> # Conversation Questions B
>
> 1. What's your first language?
> 2. What's your address?
> 3. Are you a child or an adult?
> 4. What are they? ➡
> 5. Is the light on or off?
> 6. Thank you!
>   You're _____.

3B. Conversation Practice – Pair work

With a partner, students will practice asking and answering the questions.

Answers will vary.
4. They are animals.
6. You're welcome.

Listen and repeat.

1. /A/	2. /E/	3. /a/
K	G	am
8	3	bad
4. /yU/	5. /A/	6. /b/
you	name	bathroom
use	table	bottle

A. I am Adam.
B. He needs three bottles.
C. You are at the table.

4A. Pronunciation – Sound and Spelling

1. **Model: Say the sound several times while pointing to it.** Then say the sound and quickly read the entire list, pointing to each item as you read it. Students just watch and listen.

2. **Repeat: Say the sound and each word several times, having students repeat each time after you in unison.** Be sure to use your normal voice and rate of speed. Do one column at a time, top to bottom.

3. **Solo: Call on individuals to say a sound and its word group.** Give lots of praise.

Listen and repeat.

7. /d/	8. /n/	9. /oo/
date	nice	look
do	number	good
10. /ch/	11. /u/	12. /aw/
chair	one	lost
children	money	dog

A. The lost dog looks nice.
B. The children have one chair.
C. Do you see the date?

4B. Pronunciation – Sound and Spelling

1. **Model: Say the sound several times while pointing to it.** Then say the sound and quickly read the entire list, pointing to each item as you read it. Students just watch and listen.

2. **Repeat: Say the sound and each word several times, having students repeat each time after you in unison.** Be sure to use your normal voice and rate of speed. Do one column at a time, top to bottom.

3. **Solo: Call on individuals to say a sound and its word group.** Give lots of praise.

> **Say the word and the stress pattern**
>
> | A | B | C | D |
> |---|---|---|---|
> | — | | | |
> | | — | — | — |
> | | - | - | -- |
>
> 1. numbers
> 2. letter
> 3. hello
> 4. wave
> 5. water
> 6. thirsty
> 7. phone number
> 8. languages
> 9. enemies
> 10. children
> 11. school
> 12. work
>
> ©2020-2021 Literacy International

4C. Pronunciation – Hum and clap the stress.

1. Model the first word. Say "numbers," then hum the B pattern and say "numbers, B."
2. Repeat: students repeat words after you in unison.
3. Solo: call on individuals to say the words and pattern letters.

Answers:
1. numbers, B
2. letter, B
3. hello, C
4. wave, A
5. water, B
6. thirsty, B
7. phone number, D
8. languages, D
9. enemies, D
10. children, B
11. school, A
12. work, A

> # God is Love
> 1 John 4:16 ERV
>
> So we know the love that God has for us, and we trust that love.
>
> God is love. Everyone who lives in love lives in God, and God lives in them.

5A: Bible Reading

A. Ask "What do you see in this picture?"
B. Read the verse out loud to the class in English.
C. If students ask about specific words, give simple definitions or translate.
D. Ask volunteers to read aloud sentences.
E. Ask if they have any questions or comments about the verse or picture. The picture is a father who loves and forgives his son.

> **God loves you.**
> Luke 15:20 ERV
>
> While the son was still a long way off, his father saw him coming and felt sorry for him. So he ran to him and hugged and kissed him.

5B. Bible Reading:

A. Ask "What do you see in this picture?"
B. Read the verse out loud to the class in English.
C. If students ask about specific words, give simple definitions or translate.
D. Ask volunteers to read aloud sentences.
E. Ask if there are any questions or comments about the verse.
F. **Act out the story,** using gestures to express **saw, ran, hugged** and **kissed.**

> **God is our Father**
> Matthew 6:9
>
> So this is how you should pray: "Our Father in heaven, we pray that your name will always be kept holy."

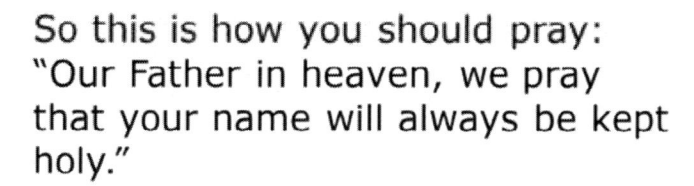

5C. Bible Reading:

A. Ask "What do you see in this picture?"
B. Read the verse out loud to the class in English.
C. If students ask about specific words, give simple definitions or translate.
D. Ask volunteers to read aloud sentences.
E. Ask if they have any questions or comments about the verse or picture. The picture is Jesus praying to his father, God.

> **God is Good**
> **Psalm 116:5 and 147:1**
>
> The LORD is good and merciful; our God is so kind.
> Psalm 116:5
>
> Praise the LORD because he is good. Sing praises to our God. It is good and pleasant to praise him.
> Psalm 147:1

5D. Bible reading:

A. Ask "What do you see in this picture?"
B. Read the verses out loud to the class in English.
C. If students ask about specific words, give simple definitions or translate.
D. Ask volunteers to read aloud sentences.
E. Ask if they have any questions or comments about the verses or picture.

God is our Creator.
From Genesis chapter 1

God created the sky and the earth.
God created animals.

Last, he created people, as man and woman, to be like Him. He told them to have many children.

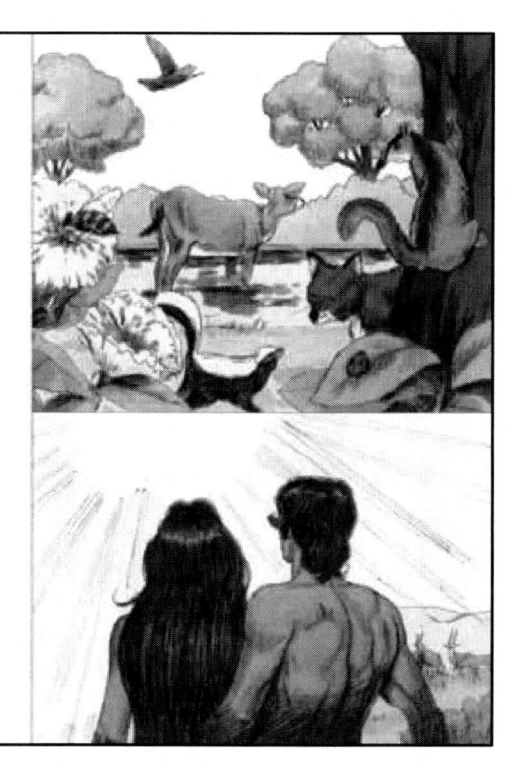

5E. Bible reading:

A. Ask "What do you see in these pictures?"
B. Read the verses out loud to the class in English.
C. If students ask about specific words, give simple definitions or translate.
D. Ask volunteers to read aloud sentences.
E. Ask if they have any questions or comments about the verses or pictures.

God is light
1 John 1:5

We heard the true teaching from God. Now we tell it to you: God is light, and in him there is no darkness. ERV

5F. Bible Reading:

A. Ask "What do you see in this picture?"
B. Read the verse out loud to the class in English.
C. If students ask about specific words, give simple definitions or translate.
D. Ask volunteers to read aloud sentences.
E. Ask if they have any questions or comments about the verses or picture.

Listen and write.

1.	
2.	
3.	
4.	
5.	
6.	
7.	
8.	
9.	
10.	
11.	
12.	

name   look
nice   789
you   do
3456   bottle
office   money
am   ABC
church   thank

6. Activities – Dictation

This exercise practices the target sounds from each lesson. Read the words and have students listen and write them. Check spelling.
1. A-B-C, A-B-C, A-B-C
2. 3-4-5-6, 3-4-5-6, 3-4-5-6
3. am, am (I am fine.), am.
4. you, you (God loves you.), you
5. name, name (What is your name?), name
6. bottle, bottle (Here is a bottle of water.), bottle
7. Do, do (Do you need help?), do.
8. Nice, nice (Nice to meet you.), nice.
9. Church, church (The boy goes to church.), church
10. Look, look (Look at the animal.), Look
11. office, office (I'm in my office.), office
12. money, money (It's his money.), money

> # Songs - Listen and write.
>
> 🔊 1. Our Lord is the ____ to ____
>
> 🔊 2. I need ____ and I need food. I need his ____
>
> 🔊 3. God ____ so good. He's so ____ to me!

7. Songs

Students will listen to the songs they learned and write the missing words.

Answers:

1. Our Lord is the A to Z
2. I need water and I need food. I need his help
3. God is so good. He's so good to me!

> First Review Quiz

Take the listening, speaking and writing quiz with your teacher.

Listen to the questions 1-7 and say your answers.
Then look at the picture and write 3 sentences about it.

Review Quiz

There are two quizzes students will take to review. **Use the Rubric found on slide 36 to score the student's answers.** The teacher will give the speaking, listening and writing quiz by asking the student the following questions.

1. What is your name? Please spell your name.
2. What's your phone number?
3. What is my name?
4. Am I a man or a woman?
5. What's your first language?
6. What's your address?
7. Are you a child or an adult?
8. Write three sentences about the theme picture. (You may show student the theme picture from slide 6 or 8 for the writing exercise).

The second quiz (found on the next slide) is online with automatic scoring. Students may do the second quiz for homework.

1 & 2 Homework

1. Read the next lesson's Bible verses: Genesis <u>1:1</u>–<u>2:25</u> in your language.

2. Take this Review Quiz at
https://forms.gle/hQxAMrB5HSVRW7qx8
and write your score here ___

If your score is not good, practice more. Then take the quiz again, and write your new score here ___

©2020-2021 Literacy International

---

8. Homework 1 and 2 – Reading the next Bible Lesson in L1 and taking the review quiz.

1. Students will always read the Bible lesson in their first language (L1) before reading it in English the following lesson. Help them get a Bible in their own language if they don't have one. They may also use ScriptureEarth.org, Bible.IS, or other Bible translation resources. The hyperlink connects to Live.Bible.Is where you can find more than 1,000 language translations.

2. Go over how to take the quiz, to be sure the student understands what to do. The quiz is automatically scored online so students can see their results. It can also be printed on paper.

If you would like to see your students' results, please **make a copy of the quiz** using the link below, and then **send your students the link to your new copy** of the quiz.

https://docs.google.com/forms/d/1Asfu37Iq2IMYVbbh3LO1e4kZ2hw0zXhGVaPEreTxwVw/copy

Encourage students to look at their quiz results and practice areas that they missed. They may take the quiz again if needed.

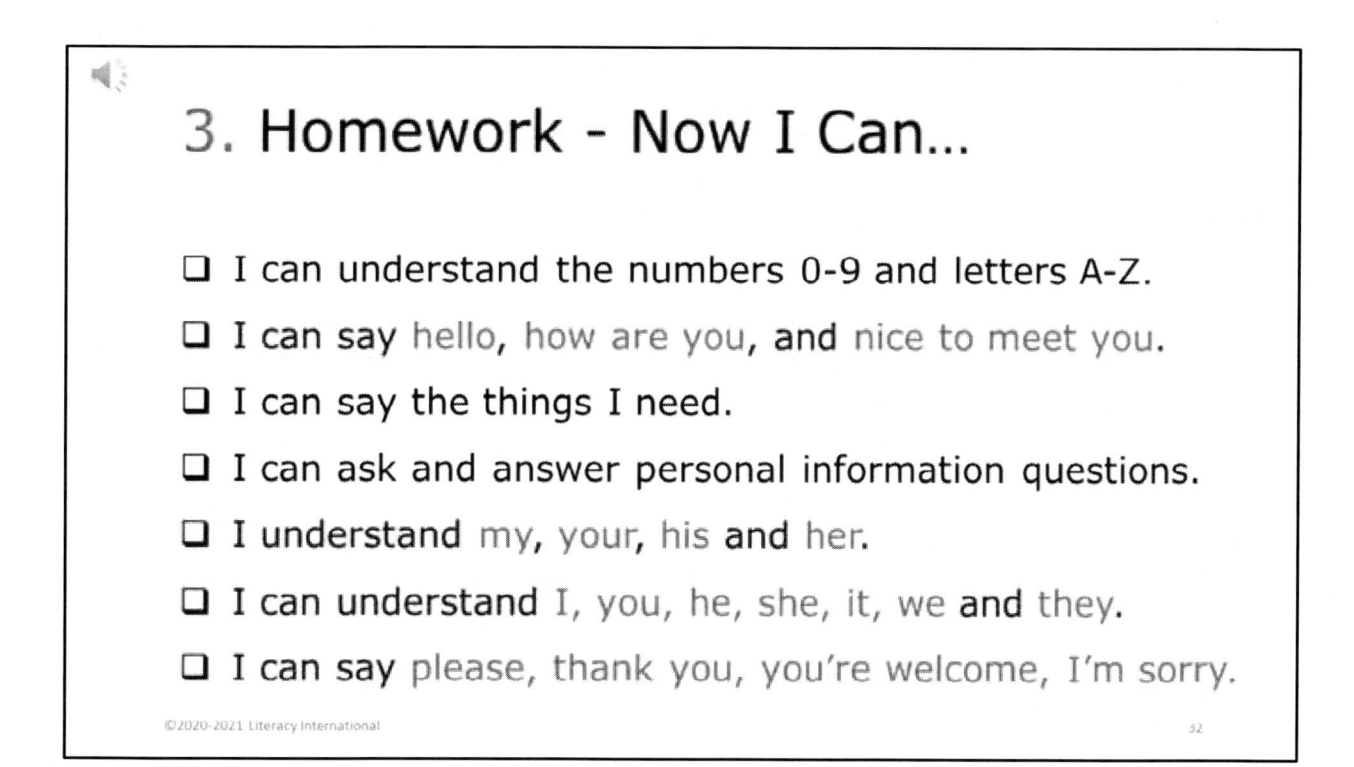

> # 3. Homework - Now I Can...
>
> ❑ I can understand the numbers 0-9 and letters A-Z.
> ❑ I can say hello, how are you, and nice to meet you.
> ❑ I can say the things I need.
> ❑ I can ask and answer personal information questions.
> ❑ I understand my, your, his and her.
> ❑ I can understand I, you, he, she, it, we and they.
> ❑ I can say please, thank you, you're welcome, I'm sorry.

Homework 3 – I can statements

The student must be able to achieve all of these skills before the next lesson. If not, the lesson can be repeated.

Review all of the skills at the beginning of the next lesson. Be sure to give lots of praise and encouragement!

Closing Prayer

Pray

You may want to ask for any special prayer requests, then pray for your students and bless them.

> # We appreciate your comments!
>
> Please let us know how you liked these lessons and what we can improve, by filling out this survey.
>
> For more information on the *Light of the World* program, please visit LiteracyInternational.net
>
> Thank you!
>
> Light of the World

Teachers and students are encouraged to fill out the feedback survey to help us improve our lessons.

Appendix

- How to Use LOTW Lessons
- Irregular Verb List
- LOTW Lesson Downloads
- LOTW Vocabary List
- Table of Contents for LOTW Lessons
- Videos

LOTW A1 Rubric for Listening, Speaking and Writing Quiz

Student Name:
Score for Listening, Speaking and Writing:
Score for Multiple Choice Quiz:
Total Score:
Date:

Listening and speaking	Question	Good - 3 points Answer is correct, clear and complete.	Okay - 1 point Answer is correct, but unclear or incomplete.	Not acceptable - 0 points Answer is not correct.
Examples:	Are you an adult?	Yes, I am an adult.	Yes. **OR** Adult am.	
	1. What is your name? Please spell your name.			
	2. What's your phone number?			
	3. What is my name?			
	4. Am I a man or a woman?			
	5. What's your first language?			
	6. What's your address?			
	7. Are you a child or an adult?			
Writing	8. Write 3 sentences about the theme picture.	Good - 3 points Answer is correct, clear and complete. Sentence begins with a capital letter and ends with punctuation.	Okay - 1 point Answer is correct, but incomplete. Sentence is missing capital letters or punctuation.	Not acceptable - 0 points Answer is not correct.
Examples:		I see a family. This is a man. They are animals.	see family. This is man they are animals	
	Sentence 1.			
	Sentence 2.			
	Sentence 3.			
Total Points out of 30				

Acknowledgements

We would like to thank the entire *Light of the World* volunteer team for their hard work and creativity in making this project possible. For all those around the world who prayed, wrote, edited, narrated, illustrated, sang, tested, and gave generously for this curriculum, we appreciate you sharing the love of Jesus through the gift of English. Our team members include:

Anonymous	Carol Hale	Tracy Meddaugh
Jean Ato	Emily Hamilton	Barbara Newsome
Larry Buell	Patty Hickman	Brenda Nielsen
Cindy Campbell	Debbie Johnson	Deborah O'Donnell
Nancy Cobb	Carey Jo Johnston	Georg Ort
Emily Cox	Nancy Kingdon	Martha Ort
Marilyn Dano	Dorothy Konadu	Joan Phelps
EasyReadEnglish.com	Martha Lane	Ellie Talalight
Don Edic	Bruce Lewis	Darrell Turner
MaryBeth Gahan	Elena Lewis	Graham Whitmore
Melina Gallo	Ward Lewis	Cheri Wilke
Alicia Gentile	Johnny Lukashevich	Ted York
Prakash Chandra Giri	Gail MacMillan	Anita Zeifert
Ellenor Gopal	Ivan Mader	
Rachel Grijincu	Amy Martin	

Bible story images by Sweet Publishing/FreeBibleImages.org
except lesson A1-29 by John Paul Stanley/YoPlace.com/FreeBibleImages.org

Learn more about Literacy International at LiteracyInternational.net

50 Common Irregular Verbs

1. Base Form	2. Simple Past	3. Past Participle
be	was / were	been
become	became	become
begin	began	begun
bring	brought	brought
buy	bought	bought
choose	chose	chosen
come	came	come
do	did	done
drink	drank	drunk
drive	drove	driven
eat	ate	eaten
fall	fell	fallen
feel	felt	felt
find	found	found
fly	flew	flown
forget	forgot	forgotten
get	got	gotten
give	gave	given
go	went	gone
have	had	had
hear	heard	heard
keep	kept	kept
know	knew	known
leave	left	left
lend	lent	lent
let	let	let
lose	lost	lost
make	made	made
meet	met	met
pay	paid	paid
put	put	put
read (pronounced /reed/)	read (pronounced /red/)	read (pronounced /red/)
run	ran	run
say	said	said
see	saw	seen
sell	sold	sold
send	sent	sent
sing	sang	sung
sit	sat	sat
sleep	slept	slept
speak	spoke	spoken
stand	stood	stood
swim	swam	swum
take	took	taken
teach	taught	taught
tell	told	told
think	thought	thought
understand	understood	understood
wear	wore	worn
write	wrote	written

Manufactured by Amazon.ca
Acheson, AB